THE SUBALTERN SUBJECT IN STRUCTURED HISTORICAL PROCESS

Towards an Epistemological Approach

Denzil Saldanha

THE SUBALTERN SUBJECT IN STRUCTURED HISTORICAL PROCESS: Towards an Epistemological Approach
Denzil Saldanha

First Published 2015

ISBN 978-93-5002-314-3

Published by
AAKAR BOOKS
28 E Pocket IV, Mayur Vihar Phase I, Delhi 110 091
Phone : 011 2279 5505 Telefax : 011 2279 5641
aakarbooks@gmail.com; www.aakarbooks.com

Printed at : D.K. Fine Art Press (P) Ltd., Delhi

Contents

Acknowledgements

I am grateful to the Indian Council of Social Science Research, Western Regional Centre, Mumbai for financial assistance that enabled me to undertake this study that was quite extensive in its coverage of sources. My young colleagues and friends at the Tata Institute of Social Sciences, Mumbai, deserve my appreciation for helping me to access a range of materials. Sumit Sarkar, Gopal Guru, Sundar Sarukkai, Ajay Dandekar and Jal Murzban were generous with their comments and encouragement and I am grateful to them. The errors that remain are entirely mine. Aakar Books, Delhi, needs to be complemented for a task that was efficiently completed.

This work grows out of an earlier publication by the same publishers: *Structure, Consciousness and Social Transformation: The Adivasis in Thane District, Maharashtra*, 2015. While the present study might be read independently, it may be seen as a companion volume to the former publication which provides the contextual and experiential basis.

Mumbai, 2015

Denzil Saldanha
saldanhadenzil@gmail.com

1.

Introduction: The Scope and Theoretical Framework

The quest by scholars for the distinctive focus of the *Subaltern Studies*[1] has been quite extensive considering the relatively long span of the writings, the different contexts, issues and historical periods under discussion, and the divergent approaches of the authors in the series; not to mention the very significant theoretical and epistemological issues raised by the Studies.[2] Contextual variation in interpretation reflecting the subjectivity of an 'elite' community of scholars of the subaltern coming from different epistemological standpoints was seen as a strength of the process by the practitioners (for example, Guha, Vol. 2, 1983, Preface). This fact should in itself have served as adequate reason to question the suggestion of the almost 'essentialist' subjectivity of the 'autonomous' subaltern subject, the 'other' to the subalternists, as seen in some of the Studies. Surely the distinctive thrust of the Studies was not the attention to the subaltern. This has been an area of interest that has preceded, has run alongside and has continued even after the discontinuation of the volumes of these Studies.[3] The consideration of the subaltern as an important, if not primary, agency for social transformation may not be seen as a defining characteristic of this historical effort. Nor has it been on the Gramscian concept of hegemony, despite the acknowledged

Gramscian inspiration of the Studies; a potentially fecund concept whose theoretical and historical exploration in the Gramscian perspective of hegemonies in contention within the Indian context could have led to a range of insights. One would suggest in the discussion that follows that this neglect of the fact of the subaltern subject as also being the contentious object of dominant, structured hegemony—in the legitimate concern to uncover the distinctive significance of the subaltern as historical agent—has resulted in a loss to holism of analysis. Holism in the analysis of systems, social formations and interrelations, it has been suggested, is one of the central features of the marxian approach (Ollman 1976: 17, 22-23, 25, 64-65, 265-266). This criterion will be the central focus of one's critical appreciation of the *Subaltern Studies* in an attempt to uncover the nature, relevance, the role of and the methodological approach to subaltern subjectivity in social transformatory processes within given social structures. One has accordingly suggested below a tentative conceptual framework as regards the epistemological approach to holistic analysis which will hopefully serve to present and assess the writings of the *Subaltern Studies* on the peasantry.

It could be justifiably argued that the predominant thrust of these Studies has been the attempt to uncover the subjectivity of the subaltern for purposes of historical analysis and thus reinstate its relative place as a historical agent for social transformation. Guha (1983 b: 13) in *Elementary Aspects of Peasant Insurgency* affirms that "it is rebel consciousness which will be allowed to dominate the present exercise. We want to emphasize its sovereignty, its consistency and its logic in order to compensate for its absence from the literature...". The relation between subjectivity, the political consciousness of the subaltern, and its agency and actions in historical processes of social transformation has been the highly relevant central concern of these Studies. However 'inchoate and naive state of consciousness' of the peasantry during the first three quarters of British rule, it is proposed "to focus on this consciousness as our central theme, because it is not possible to make sense of the experience of insurgency merely as a history of events without a subject" (Guha 1983 b: 11, also 4). This interest of the Studies has creditably called for seeking out newer sources of evidence such as oral history, memory and the over turned, 'against the grain' interpretation of scripted historical sources which might have been written by elites; innovative modes of analysis such as the use of semiotics, and a diverse arena of relatively less studied political articulations and resistance such as popular religion, spirit possession and appeals to the supernatural; rumours, legends and myths; forest fires and the preservation of sacred groves; moral outrage and even silences. The additionally stated attempt of these Studies, irrespective of the merits of the case, to confront the neo-colonialist, neo-nationalist, the enlightenment rationalist and the marxian economic deterministic modes of historiography referred to by O'Hanlon (1988: 190), one considers as derived from the above mentioned central thrust. Already during the second conference of the group held in Calcutta in 1986, Hardiman could sense that the project was at a crossroads, "One road leads towards greater concentration on textual analysis and a stress on the relativity of all knowledge; another towards the study of subaltern consciousness and action so as to forward the struggle for a socialist society" (1986: 290). Anyhow, an assessment of the contribution of the Studies to the critical historiographical enterprise that moves away from the approaches mentioned above and into post-modernism and post-structuralism is beyond the scope of my competence and of this study. I would rather concentrate from a marxian and Gramscian perspective on the aspect of subjectivity-consciousness which brings history closer to other disciplines in the social sciences, especially sociology, as regards methodology; despite the obvious differences in emphasis as regards temporal analysis. Subjectivity in this context is understood as the entire arena of human consciousness; what people think, experience and create, inclusive of culture, language, religion and the entire range of other symbolic systems of communication that influences collective action within a social transformatory process. One would also like to draw on one's historical and contemporary sociological study of a process of social change among tribals covering close to 200 years from 1818 to the present in the then Thane district, Maharashtra (Saldanha 1984/2015).[4] The study was also conducted from an attempted subaltern perspective of the tribals/adivasis in the region, relatively independent from the *Subaltern Studies* due to temporal factors of the period of its initiation and completion, and might serve as a useful reference point for the critical appreciation of the latter. The comparative emphasis would be on epistemological assumptions rather than on substantive historical content and outcomes.

In the introduction to E.P. Thompson's *The Poverty of Theory* (2010) written in 1978, Dorothy Thompson states that the book may not be seen as a definitive work of theory but as a rapidly written polemical exercise against what he understood as Althusser's idealism in its critique of historicism and empiricism and the negative influence that it was having within historical scholarship. One has, however, found the work to be loaded with theoretical insights into historical materialism; a term that Thompson preferred his work to be described by as a contributor to a marxian tradition, rather than a definitive marxist theoretical system. One will be drawing on these insights without being distracted by the question of their relevance to a critique of Althusser. Another important reference point for one's efforts will be the more theoretical writings of Sumit Sarkar, an earlier member of the *Subaltern Studies* collective and a sympathizer of the radical Left 'histories from below' that was a characteristic of Thompson and the social histories of the 1960s and the 70s. One will also concentrate on the subaltern writings and commentaries on the peasantry and the emerging industrial working class that have greater theoretical and methodological significance, even though some of the excluded writings might have uncovered valuable empirical material of a historical significance.

The three overlapping and interrelated aspects of a social phenomenon in the process of change as elaborated in the paragraphs that follow are offered for facility of presentation of analytically articulated dimensions that are holistic in character in practice, since they relate to aspects of unitary social formations in process. The three aspects are discussed at a general, abstract, philosophical level, moving onwards to a more concrete operationalization of each level. The three dimensional conceptual framework also serves as a pragmatic device in the three chapters that follow to organize and present the several fruitful insights of the many authors of the *Subaltern Studies* with their diverse theoretical orientations, as well as to undertake a critical appreciation of other commentaries of the writings. In doing so, one hopes that the distinctive characteristics of each dimension would be further elaborated, yet the need to view them as part of an epistemological holistic approach to the totality of a given social situation in tension would at the same time be underscored. Not stating this at the outset would imply falling into a similar problematic situation that one suggests has been a matter of concern as regards the Studies. This is also not to suggest that the authors discussed below within a given chapter have an analytical focus exclusively on that aspect of social reality. The concluding chapter attempts to pull together the analysis of the three dimensions discussed below within a theoretical analysis drawn primarily from E.P. Thompson (2010). It also presents a more systematic dialogue between one's work (Saldanha, 1984/2015) and what is considered to be the founding ideological position of *Subaltern Studies* as in Guha's *Elementary Aspects* (1983 b).

One could now move to one's understanding of the epistemological approach to analytical holism and to a conceptual framework regarding the same. Social situations are constituted in reality, and hence have implications at an analytical level, in terms of being, becoming and knowing. We know our social identity through the process of discovering our ontological being through the historical process of becoming. Social science analyses of human situations, if they are to do justice to these contexts, need to bear in mind the articulated character of this triangulated total reality and adopt a holistic approach; at least as a broad frame of reference if not always when undertaking contingent, focused academic practice or publication. A holistic unified approach can strictly speaking and in a pure form be conceptualized and achieved in an abstract, theoretical manner; as one's basic epistemological assumptions. The focus on the historical particular has necessarily to be contextualized and consequently bear traces of the specific and the sectorially disparate. However, it is possible to bear in mind the whole as the 'ground' when one concentrates on the 'figure', to put things in a Gestaltic manner. In fact, in the case of an analysis of subaltern consciousness, aspects of contextualized structure and historical process can serve as an important corrective during the process of interpretation. At an initial level of abstraction, moving on to the concrete, the diagrammatic illustration given below might contribute to greater clarity:

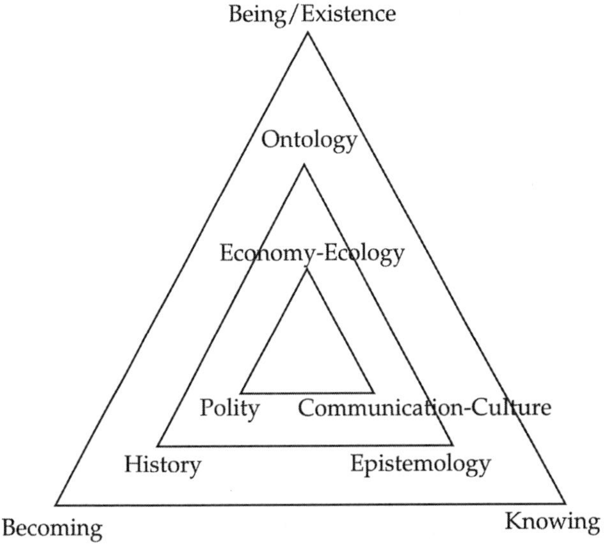

The three paragraphs that follow serve to uncover the concrete details of each of the three convergent dimensions within what is in effect a suggested unitary framework for analysis. The following chapter presents subaltern material that primarily relates to the first dimension: the social ontology of a given social formation which refers to the existential being of that formation. This would relate to the analysis of a social phenomenon as a given, as it exists as a social spatial system or the social contextual/situational aspect of that reality; a system in its relatively static aspect of factual being as different from in the process of becoming which would be the subject of the next related dimension. In *The German Ideology* Marx and Engels observe that individuals find their conditions of existence predestined, become subsumed under it (1976: 53). One might also call to mind in this context Marx's statement in *The Preface to a Critique of the Political Economy* (1977) that, "In the social production which men carry on, they enter into definite relations that are indispensable and independent of their will; these relations of production correspond to a definite stage of development of their material powers of production. The totality of these relations of production constitutes the economic structure of society". At a more concrete level, the sharp variations of ecological and socially structured context would necessitate a contextualization of methodological approaches, especially for the study of social interventions within these given structured contexts, whether the social initiatives be of an insurgent character during the colonial period or the more mass organized contemporary ones. Societies and communities at the micro and macro levels are structured on the basis of caste, tribe, class, gender, other identities and disparities and, at times, religious marginalization. These structured identities often tend to reinforce each other in situations of subordination. Issues related to livelihood and economic survival and questions related to 'where' and 'with whom' are significant for social transformative processes and would be covered under this dimension. The very structure undergoes a process of change over time due to factors resulting from the tensions between the dominance of the state and other 'elite' sections and their hegemony on the one hand and the struggles of the subordinate sections on the other. The ecological and socio-economic structures provide constraints to change, yet suggest a need for the transformative process itself. The ecological base has its own human and/or natural structural principles that also demand a regional contextualization of the change processes over variations in ecological regions. An analysis of the political economy of social situations would suggest that a central tension within this dimension is that between the expanding market for capital and the market for labour within different modes of production, markets being seen as a symbolic representation of economic exchange relations. In terms of the writings within *Subaltern Studies* with their emphasis on the political, structural aspects of dominance and subordination and the reality of hegemony with its implications for the autonomy of the subaltern will be covered in this section/ chapter.

The second aspect that will be discussed in the respective chapter is more historical in nature since it covers a temporal dimension of human agency intervening through a process towards the transformation of a given structured situation that is considered unjust. This dimension considers a social formation in the diachronic process of becoming, in contrast with the earlier aspect of relatively structured, static and synchronic ontological being. The process may be termed as 'political' in nature in its broadest sense because it implies the exercise of power and control over the distribution of a range of resources in a given structured situation. For the subordinate, in particular, organization becomes an important symbolic representation of the capacity to exercise power in a sustainable manner. Discussions in this section might provide answers to questions relating to 'how', 'when', 'who' and 'with whom' of intervening actors. This aspect might be analysed in a bi-polar manner, the tension between the state closely related to dominant socio-economic sections and civil society constituted of multiple formations, identities and social institutions. This section is closely related to the following since it covers aspects of mobilization and the socio-economic and socio-cultural identities that drive these transformatory efforts.

The fourth chapter relating to the third interrelated dimension of a given social formation might be seen as the central focus of *Subaltern Studies*, since it covers aspects of the subjectivity of social transformative processes; subaltern consciousness and the epistemology of both social science/ historiography and of the subaltern. This ideological dimension which cuts across the foregoing two aspects may also be seen in a bi-polar manner of a dominant hegemony in contention with a subordinate one in the process of formation. It provides the value loaded vision and purpose for actions. Values provide depth, significance, and energy to a given transformatory effort. They serve as an individual and collective motivating force. This aspect would generally cover questions of 'why' and 'for whom' the initiative is undertaken in the first place. It contributes to the relatively subjective and communicational/ symbolical aspects of transformatory processes within social systems. One would discuss aspects of theorization, identities based on caste, tribe and/or a more socio-economic character such as class, the religious and cultural expressions of subaltern consciousness, and the possibilities of analysing this consciousness in terms of structural collective mentalities; all issues emerging from *Subaltern Studies.*

In *The Holy Family* Marx writes, "It is not a question of what this or that proletarian, or even the whole proletariat, at the moment considers as its aim. It is a question of what the proletariat is, and what in accordance with its being; it will be historically compelled to do. Its aim and historical action is irrevocably and clearly foreshadowed in its own life situation as well as in the whole organization of burgeois society today" (1980: 47). One might interpret this apparently deterministic formulation of the 'being' of the class as the unity of consciousness and existence in historical process at various levels of totality (individual, collective, social system) being discussed as a unitary approach, reserving the term ' structured existence' for the first dimension mentioned above. The foregoing theoretical frame of reference for the study of social systems in the process of change could be visualized at multiple triangulated levels, from the abstract to the concrete, in the following illustrated manner; at the risk of unintentionally reifying what are seen as essentially analytical conceptual dimensions of a unitary reality. The diagrams are presented with the hope that they make for greater clarity.

A Conceptual Framework for Social Systems in Transformation

THE ECOLOGICAL AND SOCIO-ECONOMIC CONTEXT
Structure (Class, Caste, Tribe, Gender, Religion)
Livelihood
Question of Where? With Whom?

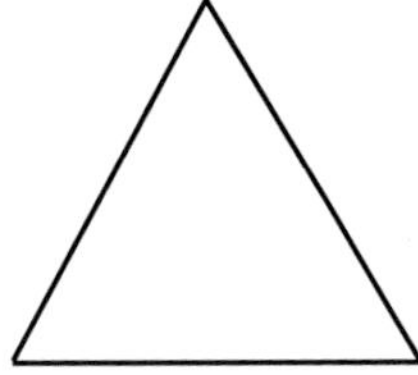

THE SOCIO-POLITICAL PROCESS
Agency (Actors)
Power (Mobilization, Organization, Strategy, Action)
Questions of How? When? Who? With Whom?

THE SOCIO-CULTURAL CONSCIOUSNESS
Ideology, Motivation, Values, Culture, Symbolic Communication
Questions of Why? For Whom?

Lest the foregoing depiction give the impression of the convergence of systemic processes in harmonious equilibrium, the same may also be illustrated in the following diagram which suggests the underlying tensions that seek resolution and which is of greater relevance to the subject under discussion: subaltern processes seeking change within given structured historical contexts.

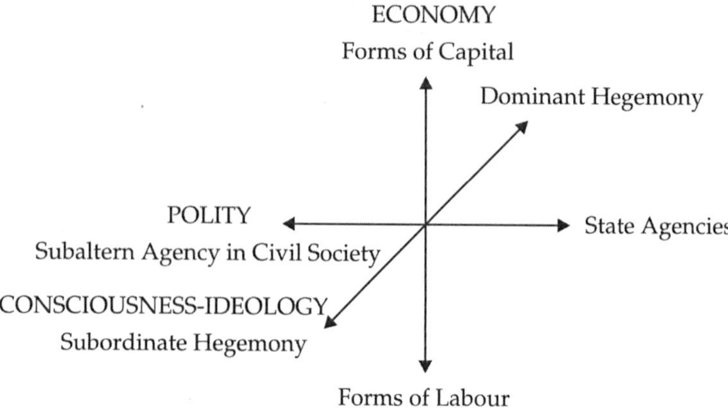

One wishes to draw attention to a certain parallelism between the conceptualization discussed above and that of Harvey (1990) in his assessment of post-modernism. What appears common is a focus on 'transitions and their subjectivity', the use of the concepts of 'space' and 'time', 'being' and 'becoming' to analyse social phenomena despite the very real differences as regards the Studies' concentration on the colonial and pre-capitalist in contrast with Harvey's assessment of post-modernist consciousness within advanced capitalism. The essential aspects of these structured, analytical frameworks have a certain similarities and could be fruitfully utilized across space and time of analytical contexts given their basic character of being generalized, philosophical and epistemological assumptions. Harvey proposes to give "an account of space and time in social life so as to highlight material links between political-economic and cultural processes...it is important to challenge the idea of a single and objective sense of time or space, against which we can measure the diversity of human conceptions and perceptions. I shall not argue for a total dissolution of the objective-subjective distinction, but insist, rather, that we recognize the multiplicity of the objective qualities which space and time can express, and the role of human practices in their construction" (1990: 201, 203). He is concerned about the representation of space and time for both theory and practice. He draws a parallel between aesthetic theory and social theory which may be considered as the subjective and objective aspects of reality corresponding to culture and politico-economic transformation; "there is much to be learned from aesthetic theory about how different forms of spatialization inhibit or facilitate processes of social change. Conversely, there is much to be learned from social theory concerning the flux and change with which aesthetic theory has to cope. By playing these two currents of thought off against each other, we can, perhaps, better understand the ways in which political-economic change informs cultural practices" (1990: 207). He goes on to write: "Aesthetic and cultural practices are peculiarly susceptible to the changing experience of space and time precisely because they entail the construction of spatial representations and artifacts out of the flow of human experience. They always broker between Being and Becoming. It is possible to write the historical geography of the experience of space and time in social life and to understand the transformations that both have undergone, by reference to material and social conditions" (1990: 327). [5] What can be positively derived from the deconstructionist critique of orthodox marxism, according to Harvey, is the understanding of difference and otherness associated with class in the process of change, viewing images and discourses as an important part of symbolic transformation, recognizing the importance of space and time for social action, and finally recognizing that "Historical-geographical materialism is an open ended and dialectical mode of enquiry rather than a closed and fixed body of understandings. Meta-theory is not a statement of total truth but an attempt to come to terms with the historical and geographical truths that characterize capitalism both in general as well as in its present phase" (1990: 355) .

One could summarize the foregoing and state in a few terse sentences one's theoretical framework. Social ontology indicates the structured character of the spatial being/existence of a given social situation. This analytical aspect is relatively static, given and seen within a synchronic dimension. The overlapping aspect of historical becoming over time suggests agency in diachronic process bringing about change in the structured being of which it is a part. As different from these relatively overt/objective dimensions, one also encounters the relatively covert subjectivity of social situations and human agency; the epistemological approaches to understanding contexts of both social science and subaltern consciousness. One might visualize human experience as mediating between social ontology and epistemology within the historical praxis of human agents. Iniquitous structures provide the ontological basis and the conditions for the possibility of an epistemology aligned to a historical practice for change of structures. Consciousness is within agents who act within structures and thus experience their individual and collective identity. The analytic configuration and convergence of these three articulated and overlapping dimensions, which might be engaged with to varying degrees of emphasis depending on spatio-temporal context and social scientific purpose, is what might be termed as marxian epistemological holism.

2.

The Ontology of Socio-Economically Structured Reality

The early volumes of subaltern writings were marked by a refreshing approach of locating subaltern consciousness and action within the material context of socio-economic existence. Evidence of this might be seen in Guha's early writings where he draws attention to the subtitle of the volumes of the Studies—*Writings on South Asian History and Society*—and stresses that "there is nothing in the material and spiritual aspects of that (the subaltern) condition, past or present, which does not interest us" (Vol. 1, 1982, Preface vii, brackets added). S. Sarkar deplores the later drift in *Subaltern Studies* from social history to cultural studies, which in itself in one's view may not be regretted, were it not for the neglect of 'material' contexts and a movement away from marxian approaches towards post-modernist and post-colonial modes of analysis as he points out (Sarkar 1997 a, Preface vii). The quest for the 'autonomy' of subaltern consciousness is seen to have resulted in ignoring a crucial element of marxian analysis: the relation to the contradictions within structures (Sarkar 1997 b: 5). He suggests that the gradual down playing of subaltern classes over the series of volumes of *Subaltern Studies* is a result of the decline of the subaltern approach: "Guha's preface and introductory essay in the first volume had been full of references to 'subaltern classes', evocations of Gramsci, and the use of much marxian terminology. Today, the dominant thrust within the project—or at least the one that gets most attention—is focused on critiques of Western-colonial power-knowledge, with non-Western 'community consciousness' as its valorized alternative. Also emerging is a tendency to define such communities principally in terms of religious identities"(1997 d: 82). And further on in the same text Sarkar writes, "Radical, Left-wing social history, in other words, has been collapsed into cultural studies and critiques of colonial discourse, and we have moved from Thompson to Foucault and, even more, Said" (1997 d: 84).[6]

Sarkar draws attention to a tendency to reify and essentialize the categories of the subaltern and its autonomy in a manner that relatively ignores the socio-economic structural contexts as a result of a fear of ending up with some form of economic determinism (1997 d: 88).[7] Authors of these Studies would generally like to locate their work within the domain of post-colonial theory. Loomba (1998: 17) draws attention to a shift in emphasis 'from locations and institutions to individuals and their subjectivities'. With respect to the narratives of gender and class, and one might add community and class, she calls for an elaboration of their articulation with each other and with social forces precisely if it is believed that human subjectivity is constituted by different discourses (1998: 241). A similar critique as regards the almost distinct identities attributed to the elites and the subaltern, but with respect to the exercise of power and dominance, is made by O'Hanlon (1988: 200). She cites (1988: 202) Gupta's reservations as regards Guha's *Elementary Aspects of Peasant Insurgency* (1983 b) where "the potentialities of a movement and its final limits are ...understood in terms of what the culture allows and not in terms of what the structure forecloses" (Gupta 1985: 10). Alam is critical of the autonomy of the subaltern that appears to spring from and flow into spontaneity thanks to a 'domain of subjectivity' that is claimed to lie in between the economic and the political and is thus unfettered by the dominant, as analysed in *Subaltern Studies*, Vol. 1[8]. This position is seen to neglect whether such autonomy of subjectivity, even if existent, has a historical impact in terms of solidarity (Alam 1983: 46). Chatterjee clarifies his position in that a domain of autonomy does not imply the absence of domination. It is precisely in order to conceptualize domination as a 'relation of power' that the autonomous identity of subaltern subjectivity needs to be asserted. "For domination to exist, the subaltern classes must necessarily inhabit a domain that is their own, which gives them their identity, where they exist as a distinct social form, where they can resist at the same time as they are dominated" (1983: 59). He further goes on to assert that the subjectivity of the subaltern as agency should not be seen in the manner of a 'functionalist marxism' towards progressive ends but as a value in its own right. Not valuing pre-capitalist, subaltern consciousness in this manner would be to condemn it to being acritical and, worse still, the reason for subjugation. In his introduction to *The Small Voice of History*, a collection of the writings of Guha, Chatterjee (2009: 13) explains that the participation of peasants in the nationalist movement was often on their own terms, for their own reasons, often refusing to participate, "In other words, the nationalist politics of the peasantry was not the same as that of the elite." A similar position of the relative independence of subaltern subjectivity from both the colonial masters and the national elites during the nineteenth century is held by Prakash (1994: 1478). It is difficult to understand how this would be in accordance with his earlier position in a joint introduction to the essays in *Contesting Power* that "neither domination nor resistance is autonomous; the two are so entangled that it becomes difficult to analyse one without discussing the other...The essays counter the notion that subaltern consciousness is either a completely independent product or that it is a mere reflection of a totalizing hegemony from above" (Haynes and Prakash, 1991: 3, 19). A similar and justifiably complex understanding of the exercise of power in society may be seen in his relevant analysis of the 'oral traditions and contested domination in Eastern India' among the low caste Bhuinyas when he writes, "These accounts of origin do not escape the language of caste hierarchy and dependent ties, but they problematize the 'naturalness' of dominance and make possible definitions of Bhuinya existence not intended by dominant ideologies" (1991: 148).

While elites are seen by *Subaltern Studies* to exercise dominance, their hold over the subordinate is considered to be not one of cultural hegemony, thus providing an arena of freedom. However, what is neglected in the use of the concept of hegemony in the Studies is that Gramsci viewed hegemony as a sphere of contention permeating everyday life practices and institutions such as the experience of production relations, family, religion and education. One's reading of Gramsci suggests that dominant hegemony is never complete, but is an arena of constant contention. He views the common sense philosophy of the masses as a consciousness that is contradictory and in contention with dominant hegemony; yet having a basic internal rationality, structured in-depth with overlapping identities, having a material basis in the natural and social environment that shapes values, and with a dynamism that is open to various possibilities. It is "the conception of the world which is uncritically absorbed by the various social and cultural environments in which the moral individuality of the average man is developed. Common sense is not a single unique conception, identical in time and space. It is the 'folklore' of philosophy, and, like folklore, it takes countless different forms. Its most fundamental characteristic is that it is a conception which, even in the brain of one individual, is fragmentary incoherent and inconsequential, in conformity with the social and cultural position of those masses whose philosophy it is... (but) at those times in history when a homogeneous social group is brought into being, there comes into being also, in opposition to common sense, a homogeneous—in other words coherent and systematic—philosophy" (1971: 419, bracket added). System change is presented by Gramsci as a struggle between unequal hegemonies, polarized around conflicting classes and seeking an allegiance from and dominance over society. The resolution of this tension would decide the direction and extent of change. While discussing attempts to achieve a standardization of thought and action initiated by the dominant, he draws attention to "a struggle between two conformisms, i.e. a struggle for hegemony, a crisis of civil society" (1971: 242). A similar hegemonic struggle at the cultural level (1971: 398) and a tension between thought and action within the subaltern is seen to result "when its conduct is not independent and autonomous, but submissive and subordinate" (1971: 327). The foregoing interpretation of Gramsci as regards hegemonies in contention is also that of Simon (1977: 78). One would tend to agree with Bhadra (Vol. 6, 1989: 54) when he writes that "the idioms of domination, subordination and revolt, I believe, are often inextricably linked together; we separate them here only to facilitate analysis. If this is true, it follows that subordination or domination is seldom complete, if ever. The process is marked by struggle and resistance". The capacity of the dominant 'to speak for the nation' (a term that is often used by subalternists in the context of hegemony) is never a coherent, comprehensive, all encompassing and conclusive voice. Even in contemporary liberal bourgeois democracy it never acquires the transparency and effective clarity of being able to silence contending disparate and dissident voices. Lack of *total* dominant hegemony does not mean 'dominance *without* hegemony', the title of Guha's article (Vol. 6, 1989) and a book (1998), but effective and adequate hegemony together with and perhaps because of appropriate and selective dominant coercion. Dominant hegemony always seeks the consent of the ruled, which does not mean that it always gets it in an absolute sense. Interpreting Gramsci in this manner helps to locate the substantive question relating to hegemony and its social transformatory role where it rightfully belongs: How come that over a period of close to two and a half centuries (if one considers the relation of the post-independence period with what preceded it; and the Studies justifiably seek to uncover this interface) there has not evolved an effective challenge to the hegemony of the rulers from within the alternative hegemony of the subaltern ruled? Was the condition for the possibility of the suppression of the sometimes sporadic, other times sustained contestations of dominant hegemony from within the subaltern, as effectively substantiated in *Subaltern Studies*, entirely due to the successful strategy of coercive dominance and persuasive seeking of consent? Or was it also due to the leadership, organizational, ideological and cultural factors internal to the subversive and mass movement practices of the insubordinate subaltern that inhibited it from comprehensively challenging dominant hegemony and asserting its collective hegemonic interests; given that one cannot expect the dominant elite to bring about radical progressive social transformation, but only pose its particularistic interests as general concerns? In their preoccupation with the dominance of colonialism and of the national elites in the process of nation formation the Studies seem to have neglected in theory the hegemonic hold of internal structural features such as class, caste, patriarchy and religious hierarchy and their relation to the colonial state and nationalist elites while ironically recognizing it in historiographical practice. The concept of autonomy, and consequently of 'dominance without hegemony', does appear to suffer from several slippages over the writings of the Studies.

The interplay between dominant coercion, hegemonic persuasion and subordinate consent is interestingly enough better illustrated by Arnold within the constraining institutional relations of colonial hospitals that attempted to confront the Indian plague of 1896-1900 (Vol. 5, 1987) and the prisons (Vol. 8, 1994). Regarding the latter, he writes: "The prison was not cut off from all contact with and reference to the rest of civil society. On the contrary, it often served an exemplary role—showing how discipline and order could, or (not infrequently) could not, be imposed on indigenous society by an alien ruling class, how a desire to overturn cultural and social 'prejudices' needed to be tempered by political pragmatism, how medicine might reign without its customary hindrances...For all its superficial isolation and its obvious physical and sociological peculiarities, the prison was repeatedly scrutinized as some sort of representative institution—in relation to caste, to disease, to labour, and to diet. The body of the prisoner and the cultural practices that surrounded it were constantly related to wider perceptions and imperatives alike among the colonized and the colonizers" (Vol. 8, 1994: 186-187). Hospitals and prisons serve as dramatic examples of institutional mechanisms seeking to dominate through coercion, though apparently in a well intentioned manner in the interest of public health and the imposition of law and order, yet able to adjust to the pragmatic hegemonic need of seeking the consent of the subordinate[9]. A similar form of hegemonic contestation may be interpreted from Skaria's narrative of literacy, in particular, and education among the adivasis in the Dangs during the nineteenth and the early twentieth century. The fixity of writing in documented agreements related to land and forest contracts, the narrowly defined interpretive community of the dominant readers and the fluidity of orality are discussed in the relation between the tribals and their colonial masters in the context of the "subaltern perception of writing as a desirable, dangerous instrument of elite domination, one that has to be both challenged and incorporated" (Vol. 9, 1996: 58).

It is a challenging task to critically assess Guha's interpretation of hegemony, especially within his thematic focus of 'dominance without hegemony' which is a constant refrain in his analysis of the discourse and practice of the dominant British and nationalist elite in relation to the subaltern. One could well interpret his brilliant analysis in the articles *'Dominance without Hegemony and its Historiography'* (Vol. 6, 1989) which deals primarily with the hegemonic character of British rule and *'Discipline and Mobilize'* (Vol. 7, 1992) that analyses the nationalist elite, as a tribute to the success of the dominant hegemonic strategy rather than as a critique of its failure, as he appears to suggest. As regards the former article, the discussion of the colonial approach of 'improvement in relation to popular dharma' and 'obedience in relation to bhakti' are excellent examples of a judicious and calibrated hegemonic strategy that served colonial purposes, even though with malicious intent. Guha raises the questions: "Why did the establishment of British paramountcy over the subcontinent fail to overcome the resistance of indigenous Indian culture to the point of being forced into a symbiosis? Why did the universalist drive of the world's most advanced capitalist culture, a phenomenon that corresponded to the universalizing tendency of the most dynamic capital of the time, fail, in the Indian instance, to match the strength and fullness of its political dominion over a subject people by assimilating, if not abolishing, the pre-capitalist culture of the latter? ... How come that in India universalism failed to generate a hegemonic ruling culture like what it had done at home?" (Vol. 6, 1989: 272-273 and 274). A brief response to these questions could well be that it was a mark of the hegemonic success of dominant capital that it could symbiotically assimilate semi-feudal formations, social relations and belief systems to its imperial goals and it did not need to abolish these relations as part of its falsely claimed civilizing mission and because Britain was dealing with a colony, and that also a late industrializing one, as different from advanced capitalism at home. As frequently discussed by *Subaltern Studies* elsewhere (for example, Guha, Vol. 9, 1996: 3), Indians were subjects and not citizens; means to another's ends. How does one expect colonial and nationalist elites closely tied to dominant interests in agriculture and that of the rising trading and corporate sectors 'to speak for the nation' (another criterion for hegemony as seen by some subaltern authors), especially to speak for the subaltern. They could only appear to, and that too not consistently and substantially, do so; and the ability to co-opt, distort and deflect the articulations of the subaltern was a mark of dominant hegemonic success. This strategy of dominant coercion combined with a semblance of persuasion could effectively draw on collaboration and offset any substantial and sustained resistance to and threat of overthrowing authority for close to two hundred years. The relevant question is: Is a critical historiography that attempts to uncover progressive social transformatory possibilities served by denying hegemony to colonialism or rather by acknowledging a dominant hegemony, however limited and distorted it might be, to it? This is apart from the issue of whether the nature of the concept in the Gramscian sense is being appropriately used.

The character of hegemony is that it functions in a grey area between contending forces and it is important that one does not get lost in the shadows. In fact, Guha's argument relating to dominance without hegemony exercised by the colonial and nationalist elite is often contradicted by his own writings. For what better assertion of the contentious character of hegemony and the affirmation of dominant hegemony might one have than his justifiable assertion, "When a peasant rose in revolt at any time or place under the Raj, he did so necessarily and explicitly in violation of a series of codes which defined his very existence as a member of that colonial and still largely semi-feudal society. For his subalternity was materialized by the structure of property, institutionalized by law, sanctified by religion and made tolerable—and even desirable—by tradition. To rebel was indeed to destroy many of those familiar signs which he had learned to read and to manipulate in order to extract a meaning out of the harsh world around him and live with it. The risk in 'turning things upside down' under these conditions was indeed so great that he could hardly afford to engage in such a project in a state of absent-mindedness... Insurgency, in other words, was a motivated and conscious undertaking on the part of the rural masses" (Vol. 2, 1983: 1 and 2). The conscious violation of codes in an act of insurgency that Guha refers to were not only those codes that were externally imposed by dominant elites and institutional relations of a socio-economic, political and cultural character, but also those internalized and introjected through a process of hegemonic, historical socialization and participation in social institutions by the subaltern. The resulting ambivalent consciousness of the subaltern—an internal conflict of consent accompanied by resistance moving towards the possibility of an externalized counter hegemony—is recognized: "Insurgency was the site where the two mutually contradictory tendencies within this still imperfect almost embryonic, theoretical consciousness—that is a conservative tendency made up of the inherited and uncritically absorbed material of the ruling culture and a radical one oriented towards a practical transformation of the rebel's condition of existence—met for a trial of strength" (1983 b: 11).[10] Conceding a contested hegemony to the dominant is not a matter of mere terminology. It has significant implications for theoretical analysis and political practice as regards the dynamics of movement from consent to contest for the subordinate.

A more acceptable interpretation of the autonomy of peasant consciousness as in *Subaltern Studies*, especially as seen in Guha (1983 b), would suggest that it does not imply lack of contextual and dominant influence; but given the different sense of community affiliations, different systems of communication, a different world view that encompassed distinct notions of space, time and causality, and understandings of punishment, "these differences allowed the subaltern classes a substantial degree of cultural and political autonomy *vis-à-vis* the statist project and politics of the nationalist elites" (Chakrabarty 1991: 2163). Their subjectivity has significance and value as a driving force in itself and it would be worthwhile to see how historical interpretation would look from the standpoint of this consciousness. Guha's *Elementary Aspects* is seen to be not an ethno history or a history of mentalities but a contribution to an alternative hermeneutics. As Chakrabarty further adds, "The fundamental problem he sets for himself in *Elementary Aspects* is: How does one read 'rebel consciousness' in a historically given colonial situation where the entire documentation of that consciousness comes from the dominant classes, the colonial and native exploiters of the peasants?" (1991: 2163). If my interpretation is right, then a relevant argument is being made to view the beginnings of an alternative hegemony, in the Gramscian sense, within colonial peasant consciousness and culture that was in contention with the dominant. However, the structural and autonomous organizational contexts of this alternative remain largely unexplored and hence the reasons for its relative failure to claim for itself its legitimate place within the nation remain unexplained. Faulting neo-colonialist, neo-nationalist and enlightenment rationalist historians for not giving subaltern consciousness adequate space in their writings, as some of the Studies seem to be doing, however legitimate this criticism might be in its own right is not in itself adequate. One sees that the rejection of meta theories and hence of holistic analysis ends up by tying some of the Studies into a social scientific bind, strangely enough at a cost to the analysis of the real significance of subaltern consciousness.

3.

History, Political Agency and the Process of Social Transformation

In his early writings in *Subaltern Studies*, Guha (Vol. 1, 1982: 4-5) contrasts the relatively vertical attempts at incorporation by the elite with the horizontal mobilizations of subaltern movements. The former drew on British parliamentary institutions and the semi-feudal ones of the pre-colonial period, whereas the latter tended to depend more on aspects of kinship, territoriality and class association. The former mobilizations were more legalistic and controlled in character, whereas the latter were relatively more violent, spontaneous and marked by a resistance to elite domination; at times taking on a sectarian and economistic character because of the diversity of its social base and the inadequacies of its leadership. He concludes that, "The experience of exploitation and labour endowed this politics with many idioms, norms and values which put it in a category apart from elite politics". In fact, most of the historical writings in the first volume, as also in the subsequent four volumes, are at pains to locate the politics of subaltern agency within the existential context of socio-material existence. One fails to understand what additional insight is provided by Chatterjee (Vol. 1, 1982: 12) by an analytical framework that identifies three 'modes of political power'—the communal, the feudal and the bourgeois—that are in effect seen to be intimately articulated with labour relations and productive processes and bear a similar more recognizable nomenclature. In a later article he clarifies that these modes of political power are located within relations of production and require independent attention given "the possibility arising of a 'non-economic' instance such as the political or the cultural-ideological becoming the structure in dominance in determining the conditions of reproduction within particular modes of production", especially in moments of transition (1985: 55). One would tend to agree with what appears to be his position that a sense of community could predominate and be an expression of a class-in-itself, especially in pre-capitalist social formations, when he later writes: "When popular religious cults deviate from the dogma of the dominant religion, when they announce the rejection of the Vedas, the sastric rituals or caste, they declare a revolt of the spirit. But the conditions of power that make such revolts possible are not necessarily the same as those that would permit a practical insubordination of labouring bodies. To question the ideality of caste is not directly to defy its immediate reality" (Vol. 6, 1989: 203-04). In this context, an article by Sarkar on the tensions with respect to caste in the self-affirmation of 'identity and difference' in the formation of nationalist identity based on Hindu identity during colonial rule and later Hindutva ideology, is relevant. He draws attention to non-Brahman movements where attempts were made to establish horizontal solidarities, embracing questions of the domination of women, in opposition to vertical incorporation. He concludes with the relevant observation: "Caste identity, after all, is not a natural, given, unchanging or hermetically sealed entity—any more than class. I have emphasized in this essay the importance of caste in the context of its relative neglect in dominant historiographies. It may be appropriate to note in conclusion that, like identities of nation, religious community, class or gender, caste does not emerge automatically, but only through determinate human praxis and discursive projections that select and play upon one or several of the multiple, changing contradictions of social life" (1997: 390).

An unjustified criticism by *Subaltern Studies* that is made of 'elite historiography' is its neglect of the contribution of the subaltern to nationalism (Guha, Vol. 1, 1982: 1, 3-4). What appears to be ignored is that the concept of nationalism is itself an elitist concept, a creation of colonial and nationalist elites in pre-independence contention. For the subaltern, as is acknowledged by Guha and others of the *Subaltern Studies* elsewhere and noted above, the concept was generally embedded in locality and autonomous governance of territoriality by way of an assertion against elite dominance. What emerges from the Studies in the early volumes is that the contribution of subaltern struggles to elite nationalist goals was in most cases inadvertent. The struggles of the eighteenth and nineteenth century subalterns persist even today as seen primarily in the tribal heartland and in the border regions, so that one might need to be open to the concept of a nation in the process of formation or a multinational nation under a dominant and hegemonic state. In his introduction to *A Subaltern Studies Reader 1986-1995* (1997), Guha draws attention to the relevant issue of whether the tension between the present nation state and civil society, both in a process of formation, "is not indeed the epiphenomenon of a deeper and basic conflict between state and community mediated by a still far from fully formed civil society" (reprinted in 2009: 332). He traces this conflict back to the independence struggles and the 'failure of the Indian bourgeoisie to speak for the nation' with the subalterns often attempting "to make these struggles their own by framing them in codes specific to traditions of popular resistance and phrasing them in idioms derived from the communitarian experience of living and working together" (2009: 329). The relevant question appears to be, with or without nationalist elite leadership, what self-consciously motivated the subalterns in their struggles and how did they interpret elite nationalist ideology; given that the functioning of colonial state institutions and its dominant officialdom were part of the lived experience of the subordinate.

Later *Subaltern Studies*, in their attempt to undertake a radical critique of economic determinism and the Enlightenment tradition, have tended to ignore movements of the Left and what might be termed as the new social movements. As Sarkar argues, "Culturalism rejects the importance of class and class struggle, while notions of civil, democratic, feminist and liberal individual rights—many of them indubitably derived from certain Enlightenment traditions—get delegitimized by the repudiation of the Enlightenment as a block....Words like 'secular', 'rational', or 'progressive' have become terms of ridicule, and if resistance (of whatever undifferentiated kind) can still get valorized, movements seeking transformation get suspected of teleology" (1997: 107 and 108). As Dirlik (1994) points out, the rejection of master narratives and of foundational historical writings by postcolonial subaltern historians ultimately results not in the contextualization of the marxian approach within the local Third World, as different from its perceived external and universalistic claims, but ironically in a return to First World discourse now in the form of post-structuralism and a neglect of the impact of global capitalism. He cites the critique of O'Hanlon and Washbrook (1992: 166) as regards the lack of a sense of totality in post-colonial writings which in effect lead to imitating colonialist epistemology: "The solutions it offers—methodological individualism, the depoliticizing insulation of social from material domains, a view of social relations that is in practice extremely voluntaristic, the refusal of any kind of programmatic politics—do not seem to us as radical, subversive, or emancipatory. They are on the contrary conservative and implicitly authoritarian, as they were indeed when recommended more overtly in the heyday of Britain's own imperial power" (Cited in Dirlick 1994: 344).

In an article that draws on a marxian analysis of the development of class consciousness in social movements, Ollman underlines the process of the class becoming auto-reflexive as part of a historical process that opens up various scenarios, not necessarily one of radical consciousness. He states, "Class consciousness is essentially the interests of a class becoming its recognized goals" (1972: 2). Despite Marx's view of 'class-in-itself' becoming a 'class-for-itself' as part of a non-necessary historical process, he suggests that there is a tendency to make a leap in theoretical analysis from real conditions to consciousness. "Marx's error, an error which has had a far-ranging effect on the history of socialist thought and practice, is that he advances from the workers' conditions of life to class consciousness in a single bound; the various psychological mediations united in class consciousness are treated as one" (1972: 7). Ollman elaborates these overlapping and not necessarily distinct mediations as recognition of interests, seeing them as collective interests; prioritizing principal interests over subordinate economic needs and as members of a particular nation, religion, race; considering the exploiter as the enemy, believing that the present situation can be qualitatively improved by themselves as part of organized action according to a strategy, and finally action especially in situations of crisis. He is at pains to assert that these contingent psychological and contextual processes are not necessary or historically determined in a teleological manner. In this context, one has reservations about Hardiman's suggestion that historians should not 'rank forms of consciousness on a scale' given its ethnocentric implications but should see how they relate to historical and social circumstances (Vol. 5, 1987: 4). Surely, both analytical processes of the development of consciousness and the changes within material history could legitimately be followed while attempting to understand the nature and contingency of subaltern consciousness. Guha's *Elementary Aspects* (1983 b) which is perhaps the most comprehensive analysis of the development of subaltern consciousness in the historical process will be discussed at greater length in the concluding section.

4.

The Epistemology of Collective Subjectivity from a Subaltern Consciousness Standpoint

Referring to some of the writings of Pandey (1991 and *Subaltern Studies* Vol. 8, 1994: 188), Sarkar is critical of the positivistic glorification of the 'fragment' in the interests of epistemological uncertainty, with a consequent loss to going into causes and contexts as part of a desirable holism of analysis (1997: 102). Pandey holds the view that the analysis of the fragment or of the 'voice from the edge' should not result in its submergence in a pre-defined whole but rather in a critique of it and a quest for alternative perspectives (2012 b: 296). He makes a strong case for a history of the everyday, the commonplace and the apparently trifling. He justifiably suggests that much of human history remains unarchived because the reigning commonsense does not consider such material worthwhile and as a result, "the archive, as a site of remembrance, doing the work of remembering, is also at the same time a project of forgetting" (2012 a: 38). To one's understanding the substantive issue is not whether the 'mad' and the 'trivial', the two cases discussed in the article, are archived or not and hence gain legitimacy. However important this problem might be from a historiographical, practical and also theoretical standpoint, the real question for the social sciences would be: What is the collective, historical and social structural significance of these apparently idiosyncratic, contingent, individual positions and their cumulative role in social transformatory processes? The social sciences by very definition engage with the process of theorization, i.e. their legitimate theoretical tendency of abstraction from the concrete and the particular towards generalization and approximation to wider analytical principles. They cannot shy away from an honest, even though tentative, attempt to address these larger questions on the grounds of avoidance of meta narratives and grand theories. The emphasis on subjectivity, new archival and other sources, on plural and sometimes contradictory perceptions may be seen as a positive contribution of *Subaltern Studies*. The question for the social sciences remains; apart from recognizing the ontological reality and significance of the particular based on the very fact that it exists other than for other reasons, how is the contingency of the particular, the individual, and even the materiality of agency to be related to the general tendency, the 'logic' of process as E.P. Thompson calls it; to the collective, and the historical structural process in order to uncover aspects of necessity/trends in macro processes of social transformation; all in the interests of providing greater legitimacy and relevance to human subjectivity in social transformation. This is a challenge for theory and political practice.

On the other hand, as Chakrabarty (1995) as also Guha (Vol. 2, 1983: 38) justifiably suggest, and if one's interpretation is accurate, marxian modes of analysis have lacked the analytical categories and the imagination to recognize the significant role that belief systems like religion play in the everyday life and the political consciousness of subaltern groups with a consequent neglect of this important area of social science or a tendency towards crass reductionism to the economic. "The problem is rather that we do not have analytical categories in academic discourse that do justice to the real, everyday and multiple 'connections' we have to what we, in becoming modern, have come to see as 'non-rational'. 'Tradition/modernity', 'rational/non-rational', 'intellectual/emotion'-these untenable and problematic binaries have haunted our self-representations in social science language since the19th century" (1995: 753). In an earlier note written as an *Invitation to a Dialogue* (Vol. 4, 1985: 375, bracket added) Chakrabarty admits: "I regard it as a still unsolved methodological problem of *Subaltern Studies* as to how we should go about creating in our work a place for this (peasant) 'experience'—given that 'experience' itself is a constructed and re-constructed phenomenon—without compromising on theoretical issues".

Articles on subaltern castes are unfortunately an exception in the series of *Subaltern Studies*. The ones by Prashad (Vol. 10, 1999) and by Iliah (Vol. 9, 1996) may be noted. Studies on subaltern consciousness are not only narratives about or even on behalf of the subaltern as the former appears to focus attention, notwithstanding the quality of the article. His analysis of the attitude of the nationalist elite to the conditions of sweepers of rationalizing the procrastination of reformist policies and taking recourse to Gandhian palliatives of hand spinning and weaving as a solution, as seen in articles in *Harijan*, suggests a useful approach of approximating subaltern conditions and consciousness through a critique of dominant mentalities and scripted policies (Vol. 10, 1999: 183). The latter author fills a major academic gap in incorporating the Dalitbahujan perspective in the writing of Indian history by drawing on his own experiences of the everyday lives and the life cycle of these communities. One only hoped that the author would have gone deeper in theoretically explaining the reasons for this gap and in relating his perspective with the historiography of some of the other authors in the series. Rao

(Vol. 12: 140ff) is a good illustration of how a holistic methodological approach to the contemporary event of the murder of a Dalit kotwal can lead to insightful conclusions. She analyses this crisis situation and the conflicting caste relations and consciousness underlying it within the socio-economic and political history of caste in the state of Maharashtra under the dominant hegemony of state policies and police as well as judicial interventions. The overt and subliminal caste prejudices are thus sharply exposed. The article by R.D. Bhatnagar and others (Vol. 12: 224ff) is another good example of the value of adopting a comprehensive approach that throws light on social structure, historical agency and popular consciousness in an articulated manner. The central concern is the contrasting and conflicting perspectives on female infanticide within a history of violence against women in nineteenth century, feudal-colonial Rajasthan. The narrative about travelling craftsmen, poets/bards from the subaltern castes of Bhats and Charans analysed in relational and not static terms helps the authors to answer the self-posed question: "Can one move outwards from the larger project of women's histories to study the poetics of bardic literature without instrumentalizing women's histories and subordinating women's issues to male concerns? The answer we found was in the affirmative: one of the gains in such a project is that the analysis of feudal-colonial patriarchies illuminates the lives of women in relation to other small voices of history" (Vol. 12: 225). The Charans are seen as social commentators whose perspectives did not always correspond to the self-representations of the elite Rajput clans and sharply differed from the civilizing mission of the colonialists. Class combined with caste analysis within the context of a particular arid geography and spatial mobility form the backdrop of the authors analysis of patriarchal history in relation to culture, as seen when the authors write, "the bard's envisioning his cultural work in the codes of artisanal guilds, and his relation to spatial location as wandering nomadic craftsmen, as well as his orientation to rural villages rather than the fortresses of Rajput power, affects the bard's ability to mobilize dissent" (Vol. 12: 239). Another valuable epistemological insight of the authors is viewing religion as mediating between history and literature in traditional Indian historical genres: "Religion is not simply an ideology, or false consciousness, or a mode of power and an apparatus for the manipulation of the masses. For our purposes, religion is also a set of conventions, epistemologies and practices which are neither predictable nor politically simple and unidimensional. It provides a set of images and narratives, and the articulation of dissent through a reworking of religious tropes by the poet-historian ...The poets and historians of a society are the vehicles of popular memory and they have the power to foment dissent. Consequently the separation of itihas and kavya impoverishes culture and cripples dissent" (Vol. 12: 260 and 279).

While recognizing the contributions of marxian labour historians, Gupta (1996) appreciates some of the neglected historiographical concerns raised by some of the *Subaltern Studies* such as the relation between the workplace and community life, and the larger themes of culture, ideology, aspects of gender, protest and deference at micro and macro levels and the ways in which these contingent factors influence the process of class formation. Chakrabarty (Vol. 3, 1984) uncovers the feudal culture that pervaded the trade unions of the Calcutta jute workers during 1920-50 as an explanation for the paradox of high and sporadic militancy with low organizational discipline. Earlier, in an analysis of the 'silences' in the records supposed to be maintained by the supervisors/ sardars of working class conditions in the jute factories, despite their efficiency in serving as intermediaries in capitalist domination, Chakrabarty writes, "What made the *sardar's* authority effective? Our tentative answer would be 'culture', the culture to which both the *sardar* and the worker belonged. In essence this was a pre-capitalist culture with a strong emphasis on religion, community, kinship, language and other primordial loyalties" (Vol. 2, 1983: 308). However, Chakrabarty's (1995) critique of Sarkar's (1977) rational, humanistic endorsement of the Swadeshi reform movement against traditional and reactionary belief systems opens up the relevant issue of what is the responsibility of a social science based 'philosophy of the philosophers' or of the 'traditional intellectuals' in the Gramscian sense, considering its legitimate wider and longer term critical perspective, towards the very real meaning that belief systems have for countervailing fundamentalist forces and for the 'common sense' of the subaltern. One's own view is that a reasoned social science of popular religion is a legitimate ideological choice based on a critically rational view of history and cannot be dismissed in a reductionist manner as a relic of enlightenment rationalism, just as commonsense based beliefs and their emotive charges may not be seen as irrelevant and insignificant for social transformation in reactionary or progressive directions. Contemporary events instigated by fundamentalist forces all too painfully draw our attention to this need. All this calls for a critical, 'organic' and closely articulated dialogue between social science and popular common sense in the manner in which both, and especially the latter, are influenced by larger socio-economic and political contexts and that as well as impact on them.

In an insightfully written piece that is *In Search of Subaltern Consciousness* (2008), Sabin attempts to relate some of the academic *Subaltern Studies* to the style of the novelist prose written about the same contexts and for the same period. She draws attention to the problems, pointed out also by others and faced in one's own work, of representing the subaltern 'other' of social science without indulging in 'self-expression', 'projections of the writer's own social position and values', engaging in 'inferences from actions' and differentiating individuals from collectives in matters of consciousness (2008: 178, 183 and 184). She compliments Amin on his *Event, Metaphor, Memory* (1995) for drawing on the art of storytelling in order to create "the impression of variety, impurity, and, finally, mystery into his story of this event" (discussed in 2008: 190). Peasant consciousness may not be seen in exclusively political terms, for the daily struggle for survival often overtakes political expression understood in restricted terms so that events unfurl through appeals to the supernatural and even madness and death, as seen in the writings of Premchand (2008: 191). On the other hand, while appreciating Amin's (Vol. 3, 1984) meticulous analysis of Gandhi's image as Mahatma as seen in rumour and popular belief, Kumar (1988) is critical of the lack of relation to the agrarian structure and political action. In a significant analysis of 'vadilcha goth' or stories about ancestors, sometimes going back to the seventeenth and eighteenth centuries among the Bhils of the Dangs, Gujarat, Skaria (1999) raises the question as to how these fables are to be viewed from the perspective of history. They are generally seen as new archival sources and incorporated into professional history or relegated to the arena of myths. The author considers these stories as a subaltern mode of coping with modernity and with history as a valid record of the past. This is through an engagement with a playful quest for values and with the comprehensiveness of truth that permits multiple interpretations of the relation between stories of imaginary gods and goddesses (devdevina) and human ancestors (vadilcha): "Maybe we should consider another sense in which imaginary goth are playful: their play in relation to the truth of khari (true) goth. That is to say, because of their independence from time and place, they are considered to be beyond the claims to truth or falsity which khari goth involve" (1999: 900, bracket added). The author suggests that the possibility of multiple fables of the same event among the Dangis goes beyond the post-modernist tendency towards the suspension of or the relativity of truth. "What is fascinating is that this is a very distinctive will to comprehensiveness: it allows in some cases at least for multiple khari goth. It is precisely this will to comprehensiveness that also renders untenable any assumption about the relativity of truth for Dangis...Subalterns, dare one say, remain haunted by truth; for them it is only too often a nightmare that will not go away" (1999: 903). A similar complex analysis of the ambivalent attitude of the Dangis to documented contracts and the written word is carried out by the author in an earlier article when he writes, "Such invocations of or confrontations with the written word were evidently fuelled by the perception that it was enormously powerful. The notion of writing as a weapon of the dominant is thus often a crucial element in the experience of subaltern groups... (seen) as a desirable, dangerous instrument of elite domination, one that has to be both challenged and incorporated" (Vol. 9, 1996: 14 and 58, bracket added).

The need for an analysis of culture and everyday life in its relation to political expressions of the consciousness of the subaltern was felt as early as the discussions towards the preparation for Volume 3 in 1982 (*EPW* Special Correspondent, 1983).[11] There have been some notable illustrations in the volumes of *Subaltern Studies*, some of them discussed above, of the analysis of subaltern consciousness and actions within structured contexts and articulated in a manner that is embedded in cultural practices. For example, Amin's (Vol. 3,

1984) analysis of Gandhi as the Mahatma is seen to gain major symbolic proportions within the consciousness of the peasantry of Gorakhpur district, eastern Uttar Pradesh in 1921-22, so that its relevance could be reinterpreted to suit existential needs and justify actions that were at times contrary to the views held by the nationalist elites and by Gandhi himself. Discussing the significance of famines in peasant consciousness in Madras during the period 1876-78, Arnold (Vol. 3, 1984: 67) writes, "For the peasants therefore famine was both an extension and intensification of familiar anxieties and hardships, and an event charged with exceptional religious significance and destructive potency. Peasant attitudes and actions were a product of these two sometimes opposing but more often mutually reinforcing elements". Famines and crisis situations served as a sort of folk calendar going back in time; markers in relation to which other events could be associated. These heightened events also entered into official records and were found useful as an indirect reference to subaltern voices which otherwise might remain unrecorded. In an interesting example of the inversion of hegemonic culture, Hardiman draws attention to the relation between values and power during the Devi movement of spirit possession and collective assertion among the adivasi/ tribals of south Gujarat in 1922-23. The commands to the adivasi gatherings of those claiming to be possessed by the Devi would relate to abstention from meat and liquor, observance of cleanliness and a boycott of the Parsi liquor vendors and landlords. "By appropriating and thus democratizing such values the adivasis sought to deprive them (the dominant) of their power of domination" (Vol. 3, 1984: 217, bracket added). In a later article that analyses the contentious relations of *Power in the Forest: The Dangs, 1820-1940*, Hardiman (Vol. 8, 1994: 146) provides a detailed and insightful exploration drawn from extensive use of archival sources of the contrasting subaltern mentalities of the Bhils and the Konkanas based on their mutual relations and their different subordinate positions with respect to the dominant colonial power. In the case of the former, consciousness and actions tended to be based on memories of former power and relative autonomy, and in the case of the latter conscious action sought political expression that was oriented to the future through affiliation to Gandhian programmes and the newly emerging post-independence political leadership.

Based on a comparative analysis of mobilizations and collective actions of the subaltern in Bengal during the Swadeshi and the Non-Cooperation movements covering a period from 1905 to 1922, Sarkar (Vol. 3, 1984: 305ff) attempts the challenging exercise "to construct a system of correlations and oppositions, structures of collective mentality conducive to rebellion or its opposite."[12] Elements in this conception that may be summarized with much hesitation are a popular perception of a real or rumoured 'breakdown' in the normal hegemony of the state that acts as a cover to its coercive powers. 'Outsiders' to the community of the oppressed tend to be the targets of the subaltern. Faced by disruptive changes in their everyday lives, resistance is accompanied by 'evocations of earlier norms'. Resistance as well as the conception of breakdown takes on a 'magico-religious character' in popular imagination. "Religion, particularly at its most popular levels, may promise the magical removal of specific ills; occasionally at moments of high excitement it can also hold out the promise of the apocalyptic vision of a total transformation" (1984: 309). Cults that accompany popular actions impose 'ritual obligations' on their followers and the 'virtue of sacrifice' especially in the leadership is held in high regard. Failure to achieve goals in a movement that has taken on religious overtones can be explained by blaming the victim and the need for self-purification. Sarkar is at pains to state that the conceptual framework that has been tentatively spelt out needs to be concretized based on possible variations. The breakdown as suggested for moments of 'popular explosion' needs to be attenuated by an attention to 'stable times'. There would be regional differences, variations over time as well as differences based on different social groups among the subaltern. The tension between the relative contributions of material conditions and the role of rumours can also lead to variations in popular perceptions. The later spread of Gandhian constructive workers as well as the Left could possibly impact on poplar perceptions thanks to relatively newer organizational and ideological expressions. Perhaps what is most significant in one's view, and which has been the basis for the critical appreciation of the *Subaltern Studies* in this article, is Sarkar's plea, "What is needed above all is an *ideal of totality*: the study of popular movement in India has to break out of the confines of the narrowly economic and the narrowly political alike, and develop into social history in the broadest sense of that much abused term" (1984: 317, emphasis added).

5.

Conclusion

The Place of Subjectivity in the Social Transformation of Structure; Dialectical and Historical Materialism as the Exploration of the Whole

The foregoing analysis would suggest the need for a framework that is sensitive to totality and the following discussion is an attempt to suggest pointers to a more holistic analysis of subaltern subjectivity; to the complex task of suggesting an approach to integrating the dimensions of the conceptualization presented in the introductory chapter and elaborated with reference to *Subaltern Studies* in the subsequent three chapters. The moving away from social history in *Subaltern Studies* towards a relatively one sided emphasis on culture to the neglect of economic concerns, as mentioned earlier, has also been critiqued by Parthasarathi (2003). While appreciating some of the contributions that are the result of discourse analysis, he holds the view that, "Nevertheless, the turn to the study of discourse, language, and representation has problematic features as well. Just as vulgar Marxism produced its own one sided accounts that reduced human experience to the economy, the study of discourse, language, and representation has increasingly come to be seen as an end in itself, in the process reducing human experience to the realm of culture" (2003: 50). The key epistemological issue for the social sciences appears to be how to hold together the dimensions of economic structure in given contexts, historical processes initiated by human agents to confront those iniquitous situations, and the subjectivity that drives subaltern actors to action. Within this totalizing framework of analysis, a related question is as regards how does the epistemological subjectivity of social science engage with self-correction through a dialogue with the 'common sense' of the subaltern, which itself is an epistemological attempt at making sense of its own realities; without substituting for or imputing a consciousness derived from social science or ideology to the subaltern.[13]

One will now draw on some of the theoretical writings of E.P. Thompson to facilitate reflection on the possibilities of a holistic epistemological approach to the subjectivity of social formations in the process of transition. This should form a useful backdrop to a more specific and systematic dialogue between one's work on peasant consciousness and that of Guha in *Elementary Aspects of Peasant Insurgency* (1983 b). The tension between structure and conscious agency with an emphasis on the latter, as Sarkar points out (1997: 54), was an enduring feature of E.P. Thompson's historiography. He has given substantial importance to the concept of 'experience' as an integrative principle in social historical writing[14]. Sarkar (1997: 63) appears to question Thompson's use of the concept of the actual, lived experience of the class as a key concept that relates structure and agency with social being and social consciousness. One has, however, found it a useful concept to understand subjectivity and the role of collective conscious agency in social transformatory processes; because experience effectively mediates between the subjectivity of the epistemological subject, which is difficult to access and can only be approximated through inference, and an analysis of its overt more objective ontological manifestations expressed through social existence/action, organization, contribution to ideology and cultural practices within structured social contexts. In Thompson's view which one will quote at some length considering its theoretical significance, "Experience arises spontaneously within social being, but it does not arise without thought; it arises because men and women (and not only philosophers) are rational, and they think about what is happening to themselves and their world... For we cannot conceive of any form of social being independently of its organizing thoughts and expectations, nor could social being reproduce itself for a day without thought. What we mean is that changes take place within social being, which give rise to changed *experience*: and this experience is *determining*, in the sense that it exerts pressures upon existent social consciousness, proposes new questions, and affords much of the material which the more elaborated intellectual exercises are about... Obviously, consciousness, whether as unselfconscious culture, or as myth, or as science, or law, or articulated ideology, thrusts back into being in its turn: as being is thought so thought also is lived—people may, within limits, *live* the social or sexual expectations which are imposed upon them by dominant conceptual categories" (2010: 10 and 12; also 137). Thompson insists on the need to engage in two dialogues: that between consciousness and being and that between the theoretical organization of historical and material evidence and the determinate character of the object of analysis (2010: 44). In accordance with a need stressed throughout this study, he asserts that, "Historical materialism offers to study process in its totality; that is, it offers to do this when it appears, not as another 'sectoral' history... but as a total history of society, in which all other sectoral histories are convened. It offers to show in what determinate ways each activity was related to the other, the logic of this process and the rationality of causation" (2010:

95). Thompson would like to term these identifiable patterns in historical material as 'logic of process' rather than laws (2010: 116). In an article that bears the paradoxical subtitle of *Class Struggle without Class?* (1978), he affirms the need for a holistic historical argument and writes that "in any given society we cannot understand the parts unless we understand their function and roles in relation to each other and in relation to the whole. The 'truth' or success of such holistic description can only be discovered in the test of historical practice" (1978: 133). He acknowledges that class may be used as a heuristic sociological category or as a historical one related to the concept of class struggle which is 'the prior, as well as the more universal, concept'. People discover themselves as classes and become class conscious in the process of struggle. "All this squalid mess around us (whether sociological positivism or Marxist-structuralist idealism) is the consequence of the prior error: that classes exist, independent of historical relationship and struggle, and that they struggle because they exist, rather than coming into existence out of that struggle" (1978: 149).

How is then conscious human agency to be viewed as intervening within the 'logic of process' mentioned above? Thompson draws attention to the "crucial ambivalence of our human presence in our own history, part-subjects, part-objects, the voluntary agents of our own involuntary determinations" (2010: 119). As regards class consciousness, he writes, "Class formations (I have argued) arise at the intersection of determination and self-activity: the working class 'made itself as much as it was made'. We cannot put 'class' here and 'class consciousness' there, as two separate entities, the one sequential upon the other, since both must be taken together—the experience of determination and the 'handling' of this in conscious ways. Nor can we deduce class from a static 'section' (since it is a *becoming* over time), nor as a function of a mode of production, since class formations and class consciousness (while subject to determinate pressures) eventuate in an open ended process of *relationship*—of struggle with other classes—over time" (2010: 143). In *The Making of the English Working Class* he writes, "class experience is largely determined by the productive relations into which men are born- or enter involuntarily. Class-consciousness is the way in which these experiences are handled in cultural terms: embodied in traditions, value systems, ideas and institutional forms. If the experience appears as determined, class-consciousness does not" (1968: 10). The development of class consciousness is seen as distancing of self from experienced determined existence in order to change conditions of existence. "The working class", according to Thompson, "made itself as much it was made" (1968: 2013).

The entire Thomsonian exercise in the foregoing texts might be seen as an effort to establish the intimately articulated, dialectical relation between the theoretical triad of structured social existence/being, human agency as becoming in historical process and, what makes this possible, conscious social experience and its symbolical products. One might recall in this context the diagram and the discussion on one's epistemological premises in Chapter 1. Holding these conceptual terms together in a holistic analysis of the unitary 'ground' of social being, as a 'conjuncture' of social and analytical forces in the Gramscian sense—despite the pragmatic relevance in a Gestaltic manner of a focus on any one aspect within the 'figure' of consciousness of social science at a given time—has bedeviled the social sciences, and one would suggest even the *Subaltern Studies*; for the over emphasis on any one at the cost of ignoring the other two related conceptual dimensions can lead to aberrations of reductionism. Every reduction involves a reification of experience and the corrective might be in not losing sight of the whole. The pitfalls are as regards the 'economic determinism' of the analysis of socio-economic structures in given social contexts, despite the fact that these contexts are socially populated by living human beings with multiple needs in historical process; with respect to the 'teleology' and political determination of historical process, despite or perhaps because of the unpredictability of human agency within defining contexts; and the 'transcendental essentialism' of conscious human subjectivity, despite this subjectivity being posited as that of the subaltern—the primary agency whose interests lie in progressive social transformation. This is because the ontological validity of the social sciences is ultimately based on a humbling approximation to the 'Truth' of a given unitary social situation that cannot be grasped in an absolute and once and for all manner, but through a process of internal, logical coherence of argument in dialectical relation with external contexts and based on a systematic gathering of information about these contexts; on a consensus about the validity of the argument at a given time and possible reliability as regards effectiveness in social intervention; especially when the subjectivity of social science is itself in dialogical resonance with the subjectivity of subaltern classes and other subaltern identities, towards ideological formulations and action.

It has been difficult to introduce one's work (Saldanha 1984/2015) in relation to the *Subaltern Studies* in a more specific and systematic manner so far, other than suggesting a tridimensional framework—articulated aspects of which one considers essential to a marxian holistic analysis—to critically represent the material of and some of the commentaries on those studies, together with my own comments drawn from my work by way of critical appreciation. The range of the studies and their diverse epistemological approaches have been an added problem and one has found this frame of reference for analyzing a social phenomenon in a unitary holistic manner to be additionally a useful device for presentation of the work of the subaltern writings on the peasantry. One's historical study in the tribal areas of the then Thane district, Maharashtra was based largely on secondary sources—from 1818 with the coming of the British, to 1944 with the entry of the Kisan Sabha peasant organization, the militant high point of the tribal struggle till 1948, the post-independence era with repression, state reforms accompanied by electoral democracy and internal class differentiation among the tribal peasantry—together with an intensive empirical study of a village in Talasari taluka of that district that was considered representative of tribal participation in the entire historical process.[15] This intensive sociological study of subaltern consciousness was carried out around 1980 and was later updated to the present. The study was carried out independently of the *Subaltern Studies*, but shares with these writings a concern for interpreting social transformatory processes with a due regard to subaltern subjectivity, consciousness and agency as mentioned in the introduction to this article. Guha's *Elementary Aspects of Peasant Insurgency* (1983 b) may be seen as providing a central ideological/epistemological thrust to the Studies and serves as a useful basis to engage with them in a more systematic manner. However, his structured interpretation of the elementary aspects of insurgencies covering the colonial period of 1783 to 1900 along the dimensions of negation, ambiguity, modality, solidarity, transmission and territoriality are so embedded in the historical contexts of the times that it is difficult to uncover the larger theoretical argument that defines the epistemological approach in *Subaltern Studies*. To that extent this classical work may be compared to the *Prison Notebooks* (1971) of Gramsci, one of the major acknowledged inspirers of the subaltern approach. Fortunately, in Chatterjee's "The

Nation and Its Peasants" (in Chaturvedi ed. 2000) we have a clear, theoretically structured interpretation of Guha which facilitates one's dialogue with these Studies and enables one to point out areas of consonance and dissonance with the predominant approach from the perspective of one's own work.

At the outset, Chatterjee states that "Guha undertook to isolate the ideological invariants of peasant consciousness and their relational unity—that is to say its paradigmatic form" (2000: 11). This relevant statement assumes further significance in the light of a noted aversion to theorization among some of the subalternists for fear of indulging in meta theories.[16] The movement of the social sciences is necessarily marked by tentative interpretative abstraction towards theoretical formulations and is a position that runs counter to the view that subaltern historiography is a quest for multiplicity, decentered identities with relatively no emerging patterns of generalization. One person's theory could possibly and legitimately become another's 'metatheory', if used in a manner that is an initial critical frame of analytical reference for dialogue with another social space and time and is open to change. It is thus that one can consider Guha's work as a relevant theoretical construct for analysing peasant struggles from the perspective of their subjectivity. He himself saw his contribution as a theoretical exercise with political significance, as "a pervasive theoretical consciousness which gives insurgency its categorical unity and helps to sort out its specific and separate moments...if the task of historiography is to interpret the past in order to help in changing the world and such a change involves a radical transformation of consciousness..." (1983 b: 334 and 336). This theoretical quest was the driving force for one's work; 'autonomous' from the *Subaltern Studies* due to the contingencies of space and time of its initial production. The present study is a post-facto attempt to address this issue of temporal dissonance and establish some meaningful relation with the Studies as regards the possibilities of substantive epistemological consonance.

Chatterjee goes on to affirm that "He (Guha) began by assuming that the domination and exploitation under which the peasant lived and worked existed within a relation of power. There was thus an opposed pair: on the one side, the dominators (the state or the landlords or moneylenders), and on the other the peasants". The foregoing conveys the impression that the peasantry was over determined by power relations and consequently suggests a theoretical interpretation of the reduction of the multiplicity of prevalent social forces to the exercise of power without going into the question of the basis of that power. One is not sure whether this is an accurate depiction of the position of Guha or, for that matter, of most of the early writers in *Subaltern Studies.* Even though the historiographcal practices of most of these subalternists have demonstrated an engagement with the more comprehensive political economy that engulfs the life of the peasantry, it does appear that some of the theoretical interpretations do suggest a formulation similar to the above. While it is true that at the times of insurgencies and at the highpoints of struggle and revolt it is the power relations that predominate and there is the stated need to draw out the political significance of a nascent and ambivalent rebel consciousness, there can be negative implications as will be seen below of this implicit reduction to power in the act of avoiding an economic one. Partly because one had taken a long-term perspective of 200 years of subaltern existence and agency within changing social formations, apart from its theoretical relevance, one has found that the analysis of peasant consciousness within the structures of the political economy provides an existential space of lived experience grounded in contrasting yet exploitatively related livelihoods and the means of acquiring them within the production process. This is in contrast with the search for a nebulous political domain/space/arena that does not have an ongoing existential basis for the independent exercise of subaltern consciousness and counter hegemony.[17] Given the relatively exclusive emphasis on the political, it logically follows according to Chatterjee that "A relational opposition of power necessarily meant that the dominated had to be granted their own domain of subjectivity, where they were autonomous, undominated. If it were not so, the dominators would, in the exercise of their domination, wholly consume and obliterate the dominated. Dominance then would no longer exist within a social relation of power with its own conditions of reproduction. In this specific case, therefore, the peasantry had to be granted its autonomous domain". One has discussed the slippages in the concepts of Guha and others of 'subaltern autonomy' and the consequent theoretical formulations of 'dominance without hegemony' at some length in a foregoing chapter. The ontological status of the concept of 'autonomy' in much of subaltern theoretical reflections suggests an independent reality, not influenced by other realities when in effect the empirical historical material that they perforce deal with conveys a multiplicity of influences on consciousness derived from the wider political economy of social forces and points, in one's view, to the need for underlining a *different* and *distinct* consciousness of the subaltern which has its own status and significance, even though not an *autonomous* one. The new questionable formulation is that of a conceptual area of the autonomy/independence of 'a social relation of power with its own conditions of reproduction'; which suggests an apparently independent, self perpetuating arena of power with its autonomous self-consciousness of the subaltern.

In an attempt to theoretically locate the autonomous political domain of peasant consciousness within the tension of the dominance of the elites and the subordination of the subaltern, Chatterjee states that "Guha was led to the study of the aspect of resistance. This did not mean that resistance was more important, or more true, than domination. On the contrary, by placing the forms of peasant consciousness within a dialectical relation of power, peasant consciousness would be assigned its proper theoretical value: its significance was to be established only in relation to its other, namely, the consciousness of the dominator". There appear to be some difficulties with this theoretical formulation. While the concepts of the subaltern 'self' in relation to the dominant 'other' does have relevant analytical value and has been fruitfully utilized in one's study of adivasi consciousness and actions in the selected region within the dynamics of state policies, the ritualized politics of electoral representation, the relation to the dominant non tribal classes and the peasant organization of the tribals and its ideology— and will be further discussed below— the above quoted statement suggests a significance of peasant consciousness 'only in relation to its other', the dominant. Apart from contradicting the notion of autonomy through its dependence on the other for its self-identity, the question might be asked, what of the additional relation of peasant consciousness to its own existential experience of a living difference from the other within production relations. In addition, if the autonomous ontological reality of subaltern consciousness is to be located in resistance, then what explains the lack of perpetual resistance and the long periods of quietude and subservience to dominant hegemony. Surely the peasantry was conscious during such phases. The theoretical stance of an autonomous political domain for subaltern consciousness and its location in resistance leads Guha to the position of 'dominance without hegemony' in order to explain moments of insurgencies.

Since the concepts of 'relations of power' or the political as an 'autonomous domain' are posited, and autonomy is located in the 'resistance' of the oppressed and seen as an expression of autonomy yet dependence in relation to the 'dominant other', and since the politico-cultural conception of 'dominance without hegemony' needs to be affirmed to suggest the condition for the possibility of resistance—all in the apparent effort to escape the economic determinism of the political economy—the social construction and constitution of the 'self' as independent 'agency' has to be uncovered. This subjective agency is found in the concept and felt experience of the 'community', a socio cultural reality.[18] We thus have a political cultural analysis instead of a political economic one. One is of the view that the concept of identity—a more inclusive and generic one, enabling the possibility of considering the existence of multiple, contextually derived and experienced identities of the individual and collective subaltern self, variably called forth to consciousness in relation to the similarly conceived dominant other—is a more fecund concept and has been fruitfully used in one's work and by some of the subaltern writers. Identity may be seen as the self perception of the individual and/or the collective experienced in a given socio-economic context and becomes the driving force for action for social transformation. Identity is experienced in relation and action in given contexts. The concept bridges and incorporates the tensions between the economic, political and the socio cultural; as objectively constituted through structured historical processes and as subjectively perceived through individual and collective socialization, organizational affiliation and consideration of the other. Identity may be assumed relatively independently by the self or be imposed by the other and introjected by the self in the context of a dominant hegemony. The concept has thus both an 'objective' structural and relational connotation as well as a 'subjective' self-affirmative one. It could serve as a fruitful conceptual modality to bridge the divide between politico-economic class and the socio-cultural community, as also to integrate the objective-subjective analytic separation. The concept of identity, to be differentiated from the generally pejorative and limiting notion of 'identity politics', also facilitates the representation of social realities in flux in terms of the narrower epistemological self affirmations of the subaltern in terms of community and/or class according to changing existential situations of struggle, and calls for a theoretical explanation of the relation between class and community.

There is no essential contradiction between the concepts of class and community. This is a view also elaborated by Sen (Vol. 5: 1987). In one's view class is not an identity that is immediately and spontaneously perceived in covert terms or, as someone said, a certificate to be carried around. However, the reality of class constitutes the ground of one's being since it is derived from the struggle for economic and physical survival; the basis of life and livelihood and hence the bottom line of existential experience. This basis underlies even the community identifications. This experience expresses itself in a community of shared culture understood in a broad sense and/or a community of shared economic interests. Both notions of community are experienced as 'self' in relation to the' other' in given historical contexts. Class identity requires organization and ideology to facilitate specific articulation. On the other hand, language, region, race, religion, caste, culture, and other gender and ethnic identities are more overt in terms of contextual practices and hence more easily identifiable and 'identity-fiable'; their 'primordial' character lending itself to more spontaneous mobilization. All these are layered, overlapping identities in the self and the perceived other at a given time; that become salient to consciousness according to context. A sense of community does not necessarily contradict class awareness, understood as a perception of shared economic interests, when it comes to a stimulus for action. In fact, community consciousness, especially when based on community organization, can act as a major driving force for action on economic and livelihood needs especially in feudal societies that may lack political class organizations.

One considers it a misreading of Guha in *Elementary Aspects* to consider the self-affirmation and the political agency of the subaltern to be reduced to a community consciousness, as Chatterjee appears to do when he writes:"In all these aspects that Guha identified, there is a single unifying idea that gives to peasant insurgency its fundamental social character: the notion of community. Every aspect expresses itself in its specific political forms through the principle of community" (2000: 13 and following). That this is not necessarily Guha's view can only be demonstrated by a number of quotes from *Elementary Aspects* of which one will present only a few significant ones. Drawing on illustrations of peasant consciousness of scheduled castes from Bengal and from among the Coorgs as also from the Malabar region during the eighteenth century, Guha writes that the authority of the 'superordinate classes' had an ambivalent value and "paradoxically enough, his (the subordinate peasant's) revolt against that authority, when the hour struck, derived much of its strength from the same awareness. Taken by itself this did not of course constitute a mature and fully evolved class consciousness. Yet it would be wrong not to regard this as the very beginning of that consciousness" (1983 b: 19, bracket added). The relation between class and community as conscious identities is best seen in terms of Guha's major contribution regarding the elementary aspects of the social 'solidarity' of the dominated, the sense of spatial 'territoriality' and self inclusiveness of the movement in relation to the exclusion and 'negation' of the other, and the 'ambiguities', 'modalities' and the modes of 'transmission' of communication during the process of struggle. A clear statement of this self conscious dynamics of the relation between class and community may be seen in this rather lengthy quotation: "Solidarity is thus a categorical imprint of peasant consciousness and there is hardly a rebellion that does not bear it. However, its quality varies from one event to another and from phase to phase within the same event depending on whether its content is a sense of belonging to the same class or any other affinity. Class solidarity and other solidarities are of course not mutually exclusive: their boundaries overlap in most cases, although the *predominance* of one or the other element would tend to determine the *basic character* of a movement. Some of the communist-led agrarian uprisings in India such as the Tebhaga movement of the share croppers of Bengal in 1946-7 and the Telangana insurrection of 1947-51—to name only two of the outstanding events of this kind—were of course distinguished by the solidarity of the peasantry as a class or to be more precise, as a congeries of classes. But even here the sense of fighting together as a class or proximate classes was over-determined to some extent by other loyalties" (1983 b: 169). Commenting on the rapidity and extensiveness of the spread of the rebellions by the Kols in 1832 and the Santals in 1855, Guha attributes this to 'a common source of exploitation and oppression' by the dominant themselves rather than to the incipient organization or revolutionary consciousness of the subordinate. He justifiably affirms that "exploitation and oppression helped to promote resistance among the peasantry long before the advent of party politics in the countryside" (1983 b: 225-26). Discussing the 'intersection of ethnic space and physical space' as part of a wider sense of class identity in opposition to the dominant other in eastern Ghazipur in 1858 and several other insurgencies, he writes "Territoriality, in the condition of nineteenth century India, helped. The reason clearly lay in *decalage,* that is, in the fact of the two kinds of space mentioned above did not quite coincide even when they converged. There were territorial units that were home to more than one ethnic group and there were ethnic regions which extended over more than one territorial unit. A peasant uprising tended, in either case, to fill in the gap by its own content and simulate a coincidence between community and habitat. An overlap of these two elements supplemented by the appropriation of one or the other by the act of rebellion was what constituted the latter's domain". But Guha hastens to add that the extensiveness of this rebellious identity still fell far short of the coverage of the nation and often acted as a constraint to total resistance against British rule (1983 b: 330 and 331).

In a similar manner, in one's historical study and especially during the empirical work of subaltern consciousness around 1980 one found that the self-identity of the 'garib adivasi' (the poor tribal, i.e. overlapping ethnic and economic identities under the organized identity of the 'Lal Bavta', the Red Flag, i.e. CPI(M) led Kisan Sabha) in perceived exploitative relations with the outsider 'panderpesha' (literally, the white-collared employer), 'shrimant seth savkar' (the rich master, landlord-moneylender-trader) at the level of the economy, took on a wider identity inclusive of other tribal groups and lower castes in similar iniquitous relations especially in moments of sharp antagonism against the dominant economic classes and the state machinery, whether during British rule or post-independence. However, the attenuating existential experience of 'rajkaran', the post-independence oppositional politics of the ritualized cycles of organized electoral participation as well as the limitations of the struggles of the peasant union, accompanied by the decline in the status and changed character of the landlord emanating from the transformations of the political economy of the region, ironically resulted in shifting identities in flux and often less inclusive of the wider subaltern. The horizontal spatial extensiveness and social inclusiveness of self identity may be seen in terms of the character of the relation to the other as visualized by the subaltern, at the level of the economy, as well as in relation to vertical political processes—of sarkar (the state) and rajkaran (electoral participation)— at a given point of time in the analysed present. When this empirical analysis of narrative material emerging from a dialogue between the conceptual categories of science and the 'cognitive areas' of the subaltern with respect to relevant social reality is accompanied by uncovering the subaltern understanding of past dynamics as explanation for the present situation and the perceived alternatives towards the future, we have a 'total conception' of the internalized collective consciousness within the individual subaltern. In one's analytical framework, the concept of identity provides a broad conceptual tool to encompass a range of existential realities and self referents in relation to the perceived other; whether they be class, caste, tribe, gender, religion, sexual orientation, region, linguistic group, organizational/ideological affiliation, etc.; depending on the contextual space, time and advance of a process of mobilization and social transformation. This concept additionally facilitates the understanding that individual and collective consciousness may be analysed in terms of multiple identities present at a given moment at various levels of depth that can be called forth to the 'figure' of consciousness in a Gestaltic or psychoanalytic manner from its 'ground', sub/un conscious according to context and the character of the dialogue of social science with the subaltern.

The conceptualization in Saldanha (1984/2015) of specific 'cognitive areas' of the subaltern of the self-'identity' of the subaltern at multiple levels (economic, ethnic, organized, strategic) in 'opposition' to the other, also seen in terms of multiple identities, and both identities (of the self and the other) visualized in differential relations to a 'totality' understood in popular terms of the 'state/sarkar' and the process of 'rajkaran/electoral democracy' resulting in an articulated 'total conception' of the present situation which emerges from a historical past towards a future alternative—of a framework to approximate subaltern consciousness had benefited from some major empirical studies on working class consciousness. Some of these studies on 'social imagery' were Bulmer (ed. 1975), Lockwood (1966), Westergaard (1970) and Mann (1973). These had been adapted to the situation of the Indian tribal peasantry through an interactive exercise of dialogue in the field. The conceptualization has been elaborated at great length in the original publication and will not be presented here so as not to distract from the main thrust. The conceptual terms 'reification', 'alienation', 'antagonism', 'participation' and the politics of 'opposition' refer to the configuration of cognitive areas in total conceptions held by the tribals, individually and collectively, varying over the historical period from 1818 to the present and according to the emerging differentiation within the tribal peasantry at the time of one's intensive fieldwork around 1980. The following diagram might contribute to greater clarity:

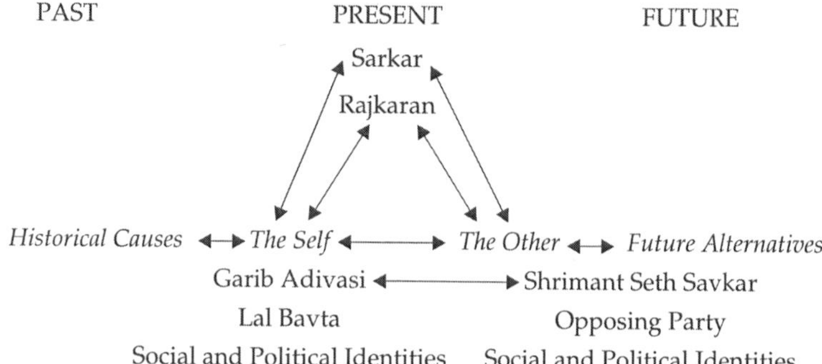

To return to Guha, one finds that the seeds of the analyzed contemporary subaltern consciousness may justifiably be found in the insurgent past, and definitely not in a demonized teleological manner, which may be seen when Guha asks, "where else except in this fragmented insurgent consciousness is one to situate the beginnings of those militant mass movements which surged across the subcontinent in 1919, 1942 and 1946? Territoriality was not indeed the stuff with which to build a revolutionary party, as Mao Tse-tung sadly observed at his base in the Chingkang mountains. But not to recognize in it the elements of what made the broader and more generalized struggles of the Indian people possible in the twentieth century would be to foreshorten history" (1983 b: 332). There is the clear need and possibility for taking a longer temporal view: At any given point of time in the past; the then historical past, contemporary present and future of the subaltern in relation to social scientist's contemporary present, contributes to an understanding of the possibilities of real future of the subaltern past. This vantage point of social science could be fruitfully utilized without engaging in teleology understood as a movement towards predetermined and necessary goals that have no demonstrated, empirical and material bases in the analysed situation. One writes this especially in the context of the apparent aversion of some subalternists to analyzing historical trends or the 'logic of process' as Thompson calls it and as mentioned earlier.

The violence of the peasantry against the 'symbiosis of sarkar, sahukar and zamindar' during the mutiny of 1857-58 in Uttar Pradesh is interpreted by Guha as a movement from an economic to a political consciousness (1983 b: 27). In one's work of adivasi self consciousness and action in Thane district, especially during the high point of antagonism against the outsider other during 1944 to 1948, one also interpreted the transition from an awareness of alienating economic dynamics to a conception of their relation to the state as 'the first glimmer of political consciousness', as demonstrated by the popular slogan: 'The sarkar and the savkar are one and the same'. An epistemological total perspective on the movement of consciousness of both the subaltern and the elite from the perception of individualized criminal violence of an economic nature between the subaltern self and the other, towards political insurgency against the state as part of the class struggle may be seen in Guha's comments on the Kol rebellion of 1832: "Nothing testifies more to the distinction between rural crime and insurgency than such recognition of the systematic, total character of the latter on the part of those to whom it was addressed. It shows that violence, confined no longer to the grey zone where the peasant met his enemy in single combat, had emerged into the open as a war between the classes" (1983 b: 160). In a similar manner that visualizes "class conflict as the core", Guha interprets the transition from the violence of individualized, covert crime/dacoity to that of collective, overt revolt/rebellion during the Deccan Riots (1983 b: 91) and the Pabna disturbances of 1873 (1983 b: 107). The process of the development of consciousness from largely economic concerns to a political perspective in relation to violence is seen in analytical terms as: "One can perhaps even go so far as to generalize that the more the violence of this type shifts away from crime towards rebellion the more it comes to be dominated by politics rather than economics, and vice versa" (1983 b: 146).

Apart from identifying the nature and structures of the systemic political economy, the character of the political processes of dominance-subordination and contending hegemonies that are prevalent; and indicating the social construction of the identity of the agency for social change; a marxian epistemology of subaltern consciousness would suggest the need to uncover the process of the transition from the individual to the collective as categories of relevant agency and consciousness[19]. Chatterjee (2012a: 14), in what appears to be in effect an inaccurate reading of the marxian position, posits and affirms a subaltern sense of community as distinct from bourgeois consciousness and is critical of the supposed reduction of the collective interests of the subaltern to a burgeois notion of a cumulative 'contract between aggregative individuals', as claimed by him. This is not the marxian/ Gramscian position of the development of a 'class in itself', an internally aggregative grouping that is structurally derived and imputed by an external science or ideology of the 'philosophy of the philosophers' to be a class; towards a 'class for itself' that is a qualitatively distinct, relatively homogeneously constituted with common interests as a result of collective action, organization, and a politicized 'common sense' or influenced by the ideology of 'organic intellectuals' of the active subaltern self against the dominant other. While discussing the cultural unity brought about by the successful resolution of the language problem, Gramsci undelines the collective as the adequate historical subject, a collective with shared and not aggregative interests: "An historical act can only be performed by 'collective man', and this presupposes the attainment of a 'cultural, social' unity through which a multiplicity of dispersed wills, with heterogeneous aims, are welded together with a single aim, on the basis of an equal and common conception of the world, both general and particular, operating in transitory bursts (in emotional ways) or permanently where the intellectual base is so well-rooted, assimilated and experienced that it becomes passion" (1971: 349). In order to underline this distinction at the level of consciousness one has differentiated the perception of 'individual needs' from the understanding of 'collective interests' and has conceptualized the introjections of 'collective conceptions' within the individual at a given point of time through an empirical analysis of the 'depth' of individual subaltern identity; apart from an analysis of the manifestations of collective political consciousness through organization, ideology, present actions and memories of the past, cultural expressions and production processes wherein individuals participate and derive their relational identity. Both individual and collective identity cannot be conceptualized outside of internal and external social relations and attributed to a single source, as Chatterjee justifiably suggests.

An important issue that emerged during one's study was how was one to think of the subject of 'collective conceptions'. Taking a class standpoint, one's understanding flowed from the very nature of classes which are units of relation structured within a larger system of relations. Classes are composed of more or less common individuals in relations and these relations give rise to shared, collectively held meanings. The relations are not only economic in nature but also cultural, symbolical and political, i.e. relations that are charged with consciousness to varying degrees; the commonality of individuals being primarily defined in terms of their relation to the process of production. Collective, conscious relations may then be seen to give rise to collective conceptions: a whole universe of meanings that are shared, commonly held and internalized by individuals differentially. They offer as it were a snapshot of individual and collective subjectivity in a dynamic process. The act of the consciousness for a class implies relations, which implies action and the social historicization of action, i.e. the historical traces that ongoing acts leave behind. An important element of the study of the subaltern consciousness, apart from collective conceptions held by individuals, would then be the study of the subaltern's culture, ideology and organization where existing, and social history within the political economy; crystallizations of ongoing historical processes. Present day cultural practices while implying a cumulative memory of the past, also contribute to future recollections. The covert processes of the collective-as-conscious can only be observed in the present in the interaction of the consciousness that takes place in collective relations, and can be empirically identified post-hoc in a contemporary sociological manner by the interpretation of individual consciousness expressed verbally. Collective conceptions occupy a significant intermediary space between individual conceptions on the one hand, and culture, collective actions, and ideology and organization wherever present. These conceptions may be seen as the theoretical and real meeting point of the scientific affirmation of the distinctiveness of subaltern consciousness and the scientific conception of the significant historical totality.[20]

One's position as derived from one's study is that the relevant human agency and consciousness in social transformative processes is the subaltern collective as discussed above. One would thus need to analyse consciousness in the context of production processes and relations, collective actions, cultural practices and ideological formulations wherever present, generally as a result of externally organized interventions in the contemporary context. The analytical dynamics is thus from the individual to the collective, from the particular 'fragment' to the relevant historical and structural whole; or the other way around. While retaining the identity of individual and collective consciousness, this inferential process is at best an approximation whose validity might lie in the coherence of the social scientific argument that is presented for academic consensus. Such an approach, it is suggested, would possibly uncover the larger social significance of subaltern consciousness and its agency in social transformative processes, thus establishing the relation between the subjective and the objective, between agency and structure and between the synchronicity of the moment and the dyachronicity of historical processes. In the living dialogue between social science and the individual's subaltern consciousness in contemporary situations, one has made a distinction between social science 'concepts' derived inevitably, but in an open ended and tentative manner subject to correction, from one's academic socialization and corresponding subaltern 'cognitions' in response.[21] Honest dialogue cannot take place with completely suspended conceptual categories of social science. These may not be considered as 'foundational' as long as they are open ended and subject to correction through interaction in field situations. Social science categories/concepts and the cognitive areas of the subaltern in response within interview situations may be considered as a dialogue directed to specific areas of social reality. The latter are also to be distinguished from the subaltern's 'total conceptions' which are in fact summative, internally coherent arguments put forward as a rationale for a world view or mentality. The total significance of the subaltern individual's 'cognitions' can be fully explained only in the context of a comprehension of the inner coherence of the total 'configuration of cognitions', in structured depth and social context. It is this subjective rationality of the individual that one has referred to as the 'collective conceptions' internalized by the individual. These total conceptions could be interpreted as being the introjections of collective consciousness within the individual, given that the subjectivity of the former cannot be accessed except through externalities. Individual total conceptions are as it were residues within individual consciousness of the individual's interpretation of and participation in intra and inter class relations. Adequate concepts and the corresponding cognitions of the subaltern might thus be seen as windows to approximate total internally consistent arguments of both social science and subaltern consciousness in communicational dialogue. The approach of discovering the collective in the individual would be in keeping with the Gramscian conception of humans as: "A series of active relationships (a process) in which individuality, though perhaps the most important, is not, however, the only element to be taken into account. The humanity reflected in each individuality being composed of various elements, 1. the individual; 2. other men; 3. the natural world" (1971: 352). One way of resolving the analytical tension between consciousness and existence would be by considering the being of reality as being constituted by these aspects at various levels of inclusiveness. An important characteristic of a marxian methodological approach to social phenomena would be a tendency towards uncovering essential processes through increasing degrees of 'totalizing' explanation. Such an approach to the study of subaltern consciousness is confronted with the task of establishing methodological links between the analysis of the subjective dimensions of individuals, of classes and/or other community formations, of historical process and the relatively objective, structural analyses of social systems in the process of change.

One's methodology and the specific operationalization of concepts have been elaborated at some length in Saldanha (1984/2015). A version of this methodology may be found in Saldanha (1988). Undoubtedly, the methods suggested for an interview or observational situation are more appropriate for contemporary sociological studies which also adopt a historical approach. The vast range of creditable historical sources and methods as utilized in *Subaltern Studies* would be suitable for both as also the epistemological approach and conceptual framework indicated here. Being historical and covering periods and actions of the eighteenth, nineteenth and early twentieth centuries, the methodological approach of *Subaltern Studies* had necessarily to resort primarily to texts; texts that speak against/about the subaltern, speak with/for, or even the few texts that are expressions of the speaking out of the very subaltern. Culture, experience, consciousness, voice/speech, language, texts and actions have an intimately articulated, mutually influencing and expressive relation with given structured historical contexts. One cannot be analysed adequately without recourse to the other. A historical study with a contemporary sociological, empirical focus had in addition the advantage of observation of actions and the interpretation of the voices of living participants in the present. One possible conclusion might well be that it helps to take a longer term perspective on the consciousness and actions of the subaltern.

Chatterjee goes on to provide a content and history to the 'invariant structural form' of subaltern consciousness as he depicts as 'autonomous community' and as supposedly enunciated by Guha as a 'formal construct'. One's interpretation of Guha in *Elementary Aspects* is that the structural form of peasant consciousness is precisely his notable contribution of the six elementary aspects which can and does change over time as regards content, comprehensive definition and with reference to sections within the peasantry; although retaining the essentials of the internal structure precisely because it is a formal construct. One might visualize similarities mentioned above with the structure of subaltern consciousness as derived in one's study in terms of the multiple identities of the self and the other in socio cultural and economic relations and in a manner perceived as articulated with the politics of 'sarkar' and 'rajkaran'. One's derived concept of 'sarkar' has much in common with Guha's concept of 'modality', as also 'rajkaran' with 'ambiguity', the perceived individual and collective 'self identity' in action analysed at various levels of social articulation with Guha's conceptualizations of 'solidarity', 'territoriality' and 'transmission', and finally the relation to the 'other' and his concept of 'negation'. This total subaltern structural conception of past, present and future possibilities is found to change in content and configurative definition in a manner that can be interpreted as a sense of 'alienation', 'separation', 'antagonism', 'participation' and 'opposition' over time and over sections of the differentiated peasantry. The analytical concepts of identity and class, precisely because of their more generic and relational character inclusive of community, can have more flexible content as opposed to the latter that tends to be rooted in ethnicity and kinship. Chatterjee further reduces the analytical concept of community to caste for its advantage in the Indian context of "the possibility of linking a history of peasant struggle with a history of the caste system, and through it, with a history of religious beliefs and practices" (2012: 16). Undoubtedly, the history of the relation between caste-class-tribe, gender and religion needs to be further explored and would provide fruitful historical insights into peasant subalterneity. He concludes his stimulating article with a relevant invitation to undertaking an Indian history of peasant struggles and consciousness in a manner related to our present and, one would add, to the history of the epistemologies of social science with respect to the subaltern.

One's general concern in this study has been as regards the question of how to weave popular culture and consciousness into dialectical and historical materialism and to do so at the same time by giving it a distinctive and relevant space; yet without setting off on a tangential trajectory of the assertion of an autonomous subaltern consciousness. The holistic epistemology of social science that has been suggested in the introductory chapter is only an approach that seeks interpretive adequacy to the total meaning systems of subaltern consciousness within systems that are viewed as structured wholes: individuals, collectives and social systems. In the analysis of the subjectivity of social processes, ambivalence and slippages, including one's own, at the conceptual level often arise from the very complexity of the subject area and some not entirely resolved questions: Whose consciousness? That of an 'objectively' structurally derived, imputing social science or the ideology of 'organic intellectuals' or that of the subjectivity, the 'common sense' of subaltern agents participating in historical processes.[22] If it is the latter, as justifiably so, is it that of the individual or the collective? If it is the latter, as the appropriate collective agency for significant social transformation, is it as interpreted from collective organizational forms, ideology, actions, and cultural practices or also as inferred from the introjections of collective conceptions within the individual in the contemporary context and at what level of depth, in which context and at what stage of a historical process; as represented in scripted documents of historical accounts and/or living, oral narratives of the subaltern self and/or the perceived other? One has found that in all this epistemological exercise of inferential representation by the social scientific 'self' of the subaltern 'other' in its own epistemological subjectivity, the ontological reality of conflicting identities within the political economy of social structure and the structure of ideological hegemonies in contention within a historical process can serve as useful points of reference and as correctives as part of a holistic analysis. The challenge before a social science of collective consciousness would be to conceptualize the link between the multiplicity and the 'profanity' of the empirically concrete, the particular, the 'fragment' and its relatively objective structural and theoretical significance. This has relevance for both social science methodology and political pedagogy. Any scientific reflection on collective consciousness brings into sharp focus the dialectic relationship between the scientist's consciousness and subaltern consciousness, confronted by the dynamic social reality of which they are a part. Given this dynamic character, we have the tension between the actual consciousness of the subaltern and the historically possible one. While preserving the relative independence of the poles of these antinomies, the relation between them needs to be brought out. Marx and Engels in the *German Ideology* explain the premises of this 'real, positive science' as: "Its premises are men, not in any fantastic isolation and fixity, but in their actual, empirically perceptible process of development under definite conditions. As soon as this active life process is described, history ceases to be a collection of dead facts, as it is with the empiricists (themselves still abstract), or an imagined activity of imagined subjects, as with the idealists" (1976: 43). At a more concrete analytical level, based on one's study and especially for contemporary studies, one has proposed the following modalities: The inferential movement from individual consciousness to that of the collective (even though it is the other way around in practice), to bridge the subject-object distinction and to arrive at the adequate agency for historical change; the movement from social relations and action to consciousness in given structured contexts; the concept of identity to draw on the livelihood basis of both class and other ethnic/cultural formations, so as to establish their mutual relations and the relation of the self to the other; to uncover the relation of the identities to state processes in order to interpret the relation between the eco-cultural in the present to the political and to the perception of past causes and future alternatives so as to arrive at total conceptions held by the subaltern within the contention between dominant and subordinate hegemonies. It is one's contention that a study of collective consciousness within historical processes of structured social change would have to grapple with the dichotomous tensions mentioned above and the theoretical implications of each of the three dimensions discussed in the introduction and, more importantly, with their relation to practice. The analytical tensions, not necessarily contradictions, discussed above may be graphically represented as follows:

Tensions in the Conceptual Analysis of Subaltern Consciousness

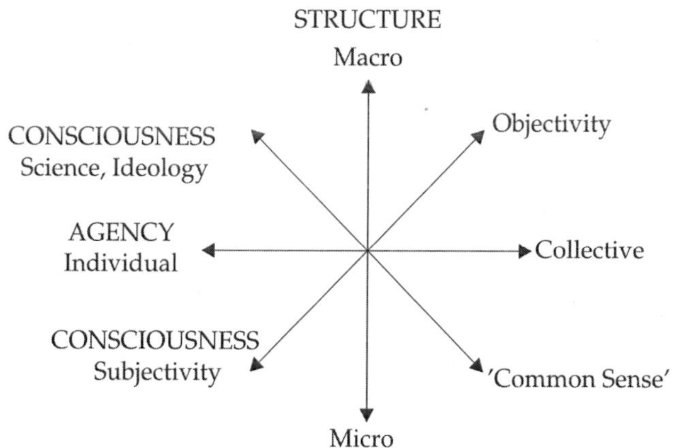

In an article that appears to be a retrospective elegy for the

Subaltern Studies, despite the disclaimer to the contrary, Chatterjee acknowledges a shift in emphasis to popular culture over time. His conclusion to the article, "Subaltern Studies was a product of its times; another time calls for other projects" (2012 b: 49), is debatable given that the 'object' of analysis of most of the Studies was the eighteenth and nineteenth centuries, 'insurgent peasant' within the paradigm of subjecthood and not the contemporary 'peasant citizen'. It is not clear whose subjective temporality is being discussed; that of the historical insurgent during the colonial period which remains the same for practical purposes or that of the participants in the Studies over the last thirty years where their situation, their analytical positions and subjects of interest would undoubtedly have changed to some degree over time from the early 1980s.

In an article entitled "Can the Subaltern Speak?" Spivak (1988) raises a basic question as regards the effectiveness of the voice of the subaltern and the adequacy of representation by social science (to the extent that one has understood a very complex communicational style). This is responded to by Maggio (2007) with another question "Can the Subaltern be Heard?", but more in the affirmative. He suggests that an effective way of addressing this issue is to understand the interaction between science and the subaltern as 'translation' and 'as a form of communication and to construe such communication on its own terms', which one understands as a critical and holistic dialogue that has been emphasized above; critical reflection together with the subaltern accompanied by self reflection of the subalternists about the subaltern, thus constituting an inter subjective community. Subaltern consciousness is an inter subjective process within structured contexts and historical processes, drawing from and contributing to the latter. So also is the social scientific process of interpreting subaltern consciousness; an inter subjective dialogue between science and commonsense. One's conviction based on one's work is that the subalterns have a voice and definitely can be heard; if only they can be appropriately listened to by social science and by political ideologists of an 'organic intellectual' variety. Listening to the voice of the subaltern has continuing value and increasing significance for both the theory and practice of social transformation. This is so especially in the present era of electoral representation when one has seen one of the greatest hegemonic manipulations of subaltern sentiment using extensive finances and all media to advantage in the context of lack of alternatives. Additionally, as Chatterjee (2013: 74-75) points out, the persistence of the peasantry of significant size into the twenty-first century, and one would add, the diversity of its subjective identities, provides a distinctive character to the Indian economy. This is a subaltern class that is being driven out of a non sustainable agriculture within the present dispensation with nowhere to go, except to what one has termed as 'industrial serfdom' and which has been so vividly analysed by Breman and others (2003, 2009, 2013) among other writings; ironically in a state that is being held up as an economic model[23]. One has attempted to suggest an epistemological approach to listening to subaltern subjectivity as both an art and a science with the hope that other holistic approaches that contribute to a counter hegemonic, subaltern standpoint will continue.

Notes

1. *Subaltern Studies* in italics or Studies in this study refers especially to the twelve volumes edited by different authors.
2. As Masselos (2002: 188) notes, "The historian is now the subject as much as what is studied". The diversity of discourses under one identity of *Subaltern Studies* in some senses parallels the diversity of perspectives within the subaltern individual at different times and within that of collective subjectivity at a given time. In the following article, one has tried one's best to approximate and accurately present the view of an author at a given time in an available publication. This has necessitated lengthy quotations at times. An added reason has been to try to avoid what one has considered a generally unfruitful debate on what the author really said or meant to say; a debate that appears to have plagued the *Subaltern Studies* more than would be justified and sometimes at the cost of substantive issues. One's approach has not been to follow the intellectual trajectory of particular authors over time, but to draw on insights from a diversity of sources and to present them in a manner that approximates a theoretical structure that one considers relevant to an epistemological approach to the epistemologies of subaltern subjectivity, to their struggles to read their world and to express themselves; the central focus of this effort and also in one's view of *Subaltern Studies*. The foregoing has resulted in references to authors based on dates of publications as and when accessible to one in the academic peripheries. In this context, the few general statements about the subaltern writings may not be seen as an attempt to 'essentialize' them, but as one's reading of a general

tendency. So much for qualifications! One has attempted to write this piece in the spirit of the "Invitation to a Dialogue" suggested by Chakrabarty (Vol. 4, 1985) on issues of major academic interest.

3. Bhattacharya (1983) provides a useful review of 'people's history', 'history of the oppressed' and 'history from below' which has a similar approach to that of *Subaltern Studies*.
4. One's study mentioned in this paragraph which will be used as a point of reference for engagement with the *Subaltern Studies* is a doctoral thesis that was started in the year 1976 and submitted in 1984 (Saldanha 1984). This study has been edited to facilitate the flow and to avoid repetition, retaining the substantial content as the same for historical reasons, and updated to the present. It was published by Aakar Books in 2015. This work formed the beginning of one's engagement with the marxian and Gramscian tradition and was followed by studies on adult education, the literacy campaigns and other educational programmes (Saldanha 1989, 1993, 1999, 2007 and 2010), among others. More specific work relating to Gramscian theory may be found in Saldanha (1988 and 2008 a. and b). One's epistemological approach and conceptual framework to subaltern consciousness that has been discussed in this work has emerged from the above mentioned field and analytical experiences of social transformatory processes.
5. Harvey provides a vivid description of the social condition of post-modernity in advanced capitalism which appears to have some similarities with the rather overstated concerns of some subalternists as applied to the colonial context: "The experience of time and space has changed, the confidence in the association between scientific and moral judgements has collapsed, aesthetics has triumphed over ethics as a prime focus of social and intellectual concern, images dominate narratives, ephemerality and fragmentation take precedence over eternal truths and unified politics, and explanations have shifted from the realm of material and political-economic groundings towards a consideration of autonomous cultural and political practices" (1990: 328). That multiple variations are possible within the 'transformative logic' of the development of capitalism is

highlighted and would be of relevance to those subalternists who appear to have an aversion to the historical analysis of enfolding capitalism under the guise of a rejection of economic reductionism and meta theoretical analysis: "Capital is a process and not a thing. It is a process of reproduction of social life through commodity production, in which all of us in the advanced capitalist world are heavily implicated... Through these mechanisms capitalism creates its own distinctive historical geography. Its developmental trajectory is not in any ordinary sense predictable, precisely because it has always been based on speculation—on new products, new technologies, new spaces and locations, new labour processes (family labour, factory systems, quality circles, worker participation), and the like. There are many ways to make a profit" (1990: 343). He recognizes that while crises in the experience of space and time may provide a necessary condition for political and economic changes, the sufficient conditions may be found in the 'internalized dialectics of thought and knowledge production'.

6. See also Bannerji (2000: 907 and following). In what appears to be a harsh criticism, T. Brass (2012: 128, 132 and following) sees a common lineage in the writings of the 'moral economists', the *Subaltern Studies* and the 'new social movements' theorists with their origins in Chayanovian populism; and "in so far as the Subaltern Studies and New Social Movements approach is structured by the increasingly fashionable methodology of discourse analysis and resistance theory, therefore, its conceptualization of ideology and action is decoupled from class and revolution. It becomes pluri-vocal, and is diffuse in its origins, causation, effect, and ultimately, in its political direction...In methodological terms, post-modernism is the mirror image of historical materialism: its unit of analysis is the individual and its sphere of intervention/determination 'the ideological' ". O'Hanlon and Washbrook, while discussing the incorporation of the subaltern by post-modernist North American scholarship, draw attention to the neglect of historicizing the emergence of this very scholarship, the ignoring of class analysis and of a critique of capitalism: "What such underclasses are denied is the

ability to present themselves as classes: as victims of the universalistic, systemic and material deprivations of capitalism which clearly separate them from their subaltern expositors" (2012: 215). They are critical of positions such as that of Prakash (2012 a) which drawing on postmodernist perspectives appear to be hesitant with 'foundational' categories derived from marxian analysis and ignore critiques of totalizing systems such as capitalism on the grounds that such analyses cannot account for variations in social formations, multiple identities and resistance: "Capitalism as most contemporary Marxist historians see it indeed constitutes a system and process but one inherently conflictual and changeful, incapable of realizing or stabilizing itself. It produces and operates through a wide variety of social relations of production and exploitation, which are themselves in constant transformation. Although its forces may shape forms of resistance, they do not predetermine its outcomes, for no hegemonic system can pervade and exhaust all social experience, least of all one that fails to meet so many human and social needs" (2012: 199). The foregoing also has relevance to the following discussion on the denial of hegemony to the dominant, as may be seen in some of the *Subaltern Studies*. Prakash's response to this debate appears to be that he is not critiquing the use of marxian analysis, but calling for a space for alternative histories that do not reduce potentially different historiographies to a subsuming into a one dimensional interpretation of the evolution of capitalism as a world system (2012 b). One is aware that one has not done full justice to the positions of the respective authors. But one's general approach to the debates discussed in this study has not been to follow the intellectual trajectories of particular authors, but to uncover what one considers relevant insights as regards the central focus on the multi-authored, perhaps faltering, epistemological quest for comprehending the nature and relevance of the subaltern consciousness of the peasantry.

7. Masselos (2002: 200) suggests that the concepts of autonomy and dominance without hegemony, as will be discussed at greater length below, can lead to a circularity of argument resulting in a disappearance of the subaltern embedded in a multi-dimensional

social context, accompanied by a focus on a questionable analytical framework relating to the exercise of power. See also Sivaramakrishnan (2002). Apart from the theoretical and analytical problems in the use of the concept of an independent and autonomous consciousness of the subaltern, there are major questionable implications for contemporary practice. As Balagopal, a democratic rights activist points out, "To break this continuum and separate the ideas of the masses from the ideology of the ruling classes requires struggle and political intervention—not necessarily from outside but not always from within either—but such a development through struggle is precisely what is denied in the notion of an autonomous and undominated region supposedly always present in the consciousness of the masses" (2002: 352).

8. It may be noted that most scholars of subaltern movements use the term spontaneous to indicate the absence of intervention of outside leadership and organization as a factual and non pejorative statement and not in the sense of impulsive and without a self-conscious reason as seems to be attributed to elite nationalist and sometimes to left scholarship by Guha (1983: 4).
9. See also Arnold's bipolar interpretation of the Gramscian concept of hegemony (2012).
10. The slippages in the concept of 'dominance without hegemony' of the elites, thus implicitly denying hegemonic rule to the dominant and consent to the subaltern while recognizing it in historiographical practice, are so often in *Elementary Aspects* that one can only attribute this to the concern to underline the supposed 'autonomy' of subaltern consciousness. See for example the inversions of signs and gestures of subordination initially imbibed by the subaltern (1983 b: 55), the contrasting interpretations of violence (1983 b: 89), the unification of semi-feudalism through the consolidation of the interests of the landlords, moneylenders and the state during British rule creating possibilities of a relatively unified conception of a counter (1983 b: 8 and 226), insurgency being seen as "a site for two rival cognitions to meet and define each other negatively" (183 b: 333). In addition, Guha's insightful article entitled "*An Indian*

Historiography of India" analyses the tensions among nineteenth century Indian intellectuals in coping with and countering the British historiography and ethnography of India, the medium of communication and the educational system. The contention within a hegemony working through disciplines, languages and educational institutional practices is clearly uncovered: "It (education) stood not only for enlightenment but also authority —a fact which it has been the function of ideology in all its forms, including historiography, to hide from the educators and the educated alike. In other words, it was an ideological effect that made both the propagators and the beneficiaries of education look on it as a purely cultural transaction and ignore that aspect that related it directly to power" (1998: 166, bracket added).

11. In one's study of tribal political consciousness (Saldanha 1984/ 2015), one has admittedly not covered cultural practices as an articulation of subaltern politics to the extent that would be desirable. This was because of one's focus on contemporary organized political expression within the larger temporal frame of the politico-economic transformations in the region, despite collecting some relevant documentation. Another factor was the length of the work which was getting unmanageable. Hopefully this will be remedied in a future publication.

12. Siddiqui (1985: 94) notes with approval the willingness of Sarkar to move freely over a time dimension, yet retaining the essential structures of popular mentality which often tend to overemphasize synchronicity.

13. While discussing the politics, culture and social life of the nineteenth century Bengali middle class and its role within colonialism, Bannerji attempts to take this unitary position in her methodological orientation: "As with the discussion on all other instances of class formation, so in the colonial-imperialist context, the social being and consciousness of a class must be analysed both from the point of view of its ontology (i.e. its formation or the objective moment) and epistemology (i.e. how it sees the world and itself, or the subjective moment). Then the structural determinations and subjective creativity both become irreducible terms in understanding class and class politics" (1989: 1047).

14. An important recent publication in this context is that of Guru and Sarrukkai (2013) that debates epistemological issues related to Dalit experience, in particular.

15. On August 1, 2014 a new district with headquarters in Palghar was carved out of the then Thane district. This district was comprised of the eight northern, less developed talukas/ blocs with a concentration of adivasis/tribals of Vasai, Jawhar, Dahanu, Palghar, Talasari, Mokhada, Vada and Vikramgad. The conclusions in Saldanha: 1984/2015 relate primarily to these northern talukas of the district with a concentration of tribals, now called Palghar district.

16. Bayly's (2012: 117) criticism of some of the *Subaltern Studies* as regards their aversion to the analysis of general trends and theorization on the apparent grounds of a fear of economism , teleology and a neglect of the voice of the subaltern is relevant in this context. Dhanagare (1993) underlines the need for theoretical analysis especially for those who would like to engage in a dialogue across disciplines facilitated by theoretical paradigms. According to Dhanagare (1993: 131), the problematic binary of 'people' as an autonomous domain in opposition to 'elite' leadership is paralleled by *Subaltern Studies* versus elite historiography (Guha 1982: 1983). Subaltern mobilizations during the colonial period are seen by the Studies to be horizontal in nature, resisting the attempts at vertical incorporation by the elites. Discussing the six elementary forms of the expression of nineteenth century rebels' consciousness identified by Guha, Dhanagare (1993: 139) finds that these are inductively abstracted relevant principles that might be mutually consistent or clash with each other and are not to be seen as ideal types of a Durkheimian character. These principles together with the concept of the autonomy of subaltern peasant consciousness and its populist influences are found to be useful for sociological analysis, with some qualifications. One would also do well to pay attention to the words of caution of Brass in the context of another discourse about populism, "Like the 'new' right (and indeed the 'old' right), the 'new' populism subscribes to a number of essentialist identities said both to predate and to be alienated/marginalized/

estranged by the discourse of rationalism. Each endorses the continued existence of many 'traditional' institutional forms linked to a supposed ability to meet basic grass roots needs. Most significantly, the 'new' populism and the 'new' right also share a belief in the undesirability of change that substantially transforms existing (='traditional') property relations" (1997: PE-33). Mallon (1994) draws attention to the tension within Latin American scholarship between anthropologically uncovering subaltern consciousness within the contemporary field and retreating to textual analysis about the subaltern in the face of post-modern radical critiques of the very transparency of these enterprises. He writes, "The archive and the field are constructed arenas in which power struggles—including those generated by our presence—help define and obscure the sources and information to which we have access. The nuance and variation in those power struggles are themselves unique forms of information" (1994: 1507). In one's study, one has experienced the advantage of in depth analysis of contemporary subaltern consciousness as part of a sociological study accompanied by a reading back into scripted historical texts and finding a space for contemporary popular interpretations based on oral narratives of the past.

17. One has found that that the concepts of 'political domain' and 'modes of power' that have been introduced by Chatterjee have some ambiguities as pointed out by Prasad (1985) and despite clarifications (1983 and 1985). So also with the concept of 'political society' (2011). While the historical and empirical details that are uncovered by some of these writings are valuable, from one's limited understanding one fails to see how the introduction of new categories provides value addition given that those realities could be or have already been analysed by existing concepts within the marxian tradition. Anyhow, it would be a deflection from the central purpose to enter into this debate.
18. Hardiman (1993: 8-9) undertakes a strong defence of community self awareness in his introduction to *Peasant Resistance in India, 1858-1914*, while acknowledging that none of the other contributors to the volume do so.

19. The writings of Goldmann (1971) have been relevant for understanding the transition from the individual to the collective in both consciousness and practice, during one's study. He maintains that the hypothesis of the individual subject cannot provide an adequate explanation for collective activity which is not the additive product of individual wills. An individual is part of different collectives at different points of time. Individual identity is composed of several overlapping collective identities of varying significance; a particular collective identity being selectively heightened in particular social contexts. Of all the collective subjects, social classes have a special status in that their consciousness and action are directed to the organization of the relationship between human beings and nature and between themselves. He holds the view that by shifting attention from the individual subject to the trans-individual subject we are able to resolve several dichotomies that plague positivist thought. The 'partial identity' of subject and object in the collective subject facilitates the understanding of self in the act of comprehending the object of which it is a constitutive part. While acknowledging the limiting influences of social structures, it permits social groups an area of freedom to change those structures. Goldmann maintains that collective consciousness always bears a functional relationship to actual behaviour, unlike at the individual level where there are complexities of personality and contextual constraints that mediate between consciousness and action. He introduces the concept of 'functional structures or significant structures'. He suggests that the investigation of these structures involves "on the one hand an internal analysis aiming to *understand* them by revealing the immanent structure, and consequently the potential significance of the various elements of a given relationship, and on the other hand, an external analysis, aiming to *explain* them by inserting the structure as a functional element in another larger structure". He identifies this mode of analysis as 'genetic structuralism'. "This means that we must take seriously the assertion that no human act is absurd, that what may seem meaningless is in reality either an incomplete fact which the researcher has mistakenly isolated from the total reality or else a mixture of different meanings related to different

subjects; a true understanding depends on either inserting this fact into a larger whole and into the historical process or else on sorting out the different elements which make up the mixture, or perhaps on both together" (Goldmann: 1971: 73-75 and 75-76).

20. This might be as good a place as any to introduce some of the ideas from the debate between Chibber(2013 and 2014) and Chatterjee (2013) relating to *Subaltern Studies* and as related to one's central focus on the epistemology of subaltern consciousness. Within the context of the debate, both tend to neglect the nature of individual/collective subaltern consciousness, its role within social transformatory processes and the epistemological issues with respect to analysing this consciousness. *Subaltern Studies* posited these questions as its central concern, but then got deflected into a post-colonial critique of third world capitalism, its dominance over the subaltern without hegemony, the autonomy of the latter, a critique of post enlightenment materialist determinism, rationalism, historicism, elitist historiography and then moved for a greater part into a tangential deviation into a post-modernist, post-structuralist and linguistic interpretation of subaltern consciousness as a corrective to a supposedly post-enlightenment marxian interpretation. Chibber, engrossed with a critique of *Subaltern Studies* and a defense of a marxian interpretation of globalized capitalism, also effectively moves away from a marxian analysis of consciousness. The Chibber-Chatterjee debate has largely concentrated on the application of marxian 'universalizing categories' related to capitalist transformation to the Indian context. Ironically, in both one sees a focus on dominant capitalism rather than a serious engagement with the strengths and limitations of a marxian analysis of subaltern consciousness in social transformation. The debate has also unfortunately deviated into questions of who really said what. While important in itself, one will try to concentrate on questions related to agency and interests which have been the subject of Chapters 7 and 8 in Chibber (2013) and the focus of this piece. Chibber makes the justifiable point that recognizing material interests does not suggest the neglect of culture and ideology in the social construction of agency (2013:

178). There is an interesting discussion on the relationship between perceived needs, identified interests and reasoned motivations that constitute human agency (2013: 187 and following). One's position is that a distinction might be made between individually perceived subaltern needs which corresponds to Chibber's 'need for physical well-being' (2013: 203) and collective interests even though perceived by the individual which Guha (1983 b: 160 and 169, cited above) acknowledges as a movement of solidarity from the individual to the collective, from the experience of the economic to the political and from the demands of the present to aspirations for the long term. One's study suggests that when individual needs develop into collective interests, both derived from multiple sources, we have a reasoned motivation for collective agency to act in social transformative processes.

21. The methodology of Lehmann(1972) in his analysis of the 'conceptual universe' of peasants during the agrarian reform in Chile had been useful for one's understanding of individual tribal 'cognitions' in relation to their 'total conceptions' and the articulation of the latter with structured transformatory processes. He writes, "These questions acquire added relevance when the object of analysis lies neither purely in the world of subjective dispositions nor purely in that of social and political action, but rather precisely at the point where the two intersect: consciousness". The problem of representativeness was handled by identifying what might be considered as generic themes relating to the sub-culture and that are often repeated. "The principal method of guarding against triviality has been to introduce order into the elaboration of different forms of consciousness, by tracing the changing relationships among a stable set of themes in three different forms of economic and social organization, the concepts chosen being wide enough in their applicability to be of relevance in all the structural contexts considered, and arising frequently enough in interviews to be of clearly central importance in the peasants culture... The object of a sociology of consciousness must be the encounter of the subjective and the objective, of concepts and specific situations,

of belief, action and social structure". Explaining his focus on the concepts that subjects use, the author writes "to understand political action it is more useful to look at the concepts which actors bring in situations than at the attitudes which are expressed on the basis of those concepts. Concepts can be assumed to be culturally 'given' and their meaning is defined by their relationship to other concepts. The analysis of concepts drawn from interviews permits their discussion at a cultural level without the pitfalls of statistical analysis. Although our unit of observation is the individual, the culture or sub-culture, is our unit of analysis" (Lehmann 1972: 296-298 and 303).

22. One might note here the sharp distinction between Lukacs' approach in *History and Class Consciousness* to ideologically imputing a class consciousness (1971: 51) to the working class and the Gramcian understanding of the significance of actual common sense as the basis for class consciousness as seen throughout the *Prison Notebooks* (1971). One has adopted the latter position. Connerton attributes the shortcomings of Lukacs' discussion to the fact that generally marxian concepts tend to be used critically and not descriptively and hence in an anti-psychological manner. He sees "a danger in this anti-psychological critique: the danger of making the psychological or whatever is subsumed under that category, quite simply historically irrelevant. The subjective, the psychological, can then be treated as a merely accidental factor in a new historical picture, in the framework of which it can be made to appear as a troublesome superfluity" (1974: 174). Connerton stresses the importance of the actual consciousness of the masses and suggests the need to study this consciousness with an approach that is a critical, psychoanalytic social psychology.

23. Chatterjee (2011) has ably described this process, except for the neglect of issues related to ecological sustainability and the introduction of the ambiguous concept of 'political society' as distinct from a narrow view of 'civil society', yet related to it and both differentially related to the state and the corporate sector. One has earlier made a passing comment on this. Breman's remarkable collection of work that depicts this peasantry as seasonal circulatory migrants, wage hunters and gatherers,

footloose labour, and unfree workforce in the informal economy underlines a significant transition that the country faces, quite unbearable to the subaltern; a transition if not from a stagnant and predatory capitalism to a more advanced and stable one, definitely a unique transition from a non-sustainable agriculture to 'industrial serfdom' as one has described the situation in a region bordering on Gujarat (Saldanha 1984/2015).

References

Alam, J. (1983): "Peasantry, Politics and Historiography: Critique of New Trend in Relation to Marxism", *Social Scientist*, Vol. 11, No. 117, February.

Amin, S. (1984): "Gandhi as Mahatma: Gorakhpur District, Eastern UP, 1921-2" in R. Guha (ed.) *Subaltern Studies,* Vol. 3 (New Delhi: OUP).

Arnold, D (1987): "Touching the Body: Perspectives on the Indian Plague, 1896-1900" in R. Guha (ed.) *Subaltern Studies,* Vol. 5 (New Delhi: OUP).

—— (1994): "The Colonial Prison: Power, Knowledge and Penology in Nineteenth-Century India" in D. Arnold and D. Hardiman (eds.) *Subaltern Studies,* Vol. 8 (New Delhi: OUP).

—— (2012): "Gramsci and Peasant Subalternity in India" in V. Chaturvedi (ed.).

Balagopal, K. (2002): "Drought and TADA in Adilabad" in D. Ludden (ed.).

Bannerji, H. (1989): "The Mirror of Class: Class Subjectivity and Politics in 19th Century Bengal", *Economic and Political Weekly*, Vol. XXIV, No. 19, May 13.

—— (2000): "Projects of Hegemony: Towards a Critique of Subaltern Studies', 'Resolution of the Women's Question'", *Economic and Political Weekly*, Vol. XXXV, No. 11, March 11.

Bayly, C. (2012): "Rallying Around the Subaltern" in V. Chaturvedi (ed.).

Bhadra, G. (1989): "The Mentality of Subalternity: *Kantanama or*

Rajdharma" in R. Guha (ed.) *Subaltern Studies*, Vol. 5 (New Delhi: OUP).

Bhatnagar, R.D. et al. (2005): "A Poetics of Resistance: Investigating the Rhetoric of the Bardic Historians of Rajasthan" in S. Mayaram and others (eds.), *Subaltern Studies*, Vol. 12 (Ranikhet: Permanent Black).

Bhattacharya, S. (1983): "History from Below", *Social Scientist*, Vol. 119, April.

Brass, T. (1997): "The Agrarian Myth, the 'New' Populism and the 'New' Right", *Economic and Political Weekly*, Vol. XXXII, No. 4, January 25.

—— (2012): "Moral Economists, Subalterns, New Social Movements and the (Re-) Emergence of a (Post-) Modernized (Middle) Peasant", in V. Chaturvedi (ed.).

Breman, J. (2003): *The Labouring Poor in India: Patterns of Exploitation and Exclusion* (Delhi: OUP).

—— (2013): *At Work in the Informal Economy of India: Perspective from the Bottom Up* (Delhi: OUP).

Breman, J. and others (eds.) (2009): *India's Unfree Workforce: Of Bondage Old and New* (New Delhi: OUP).

Bulmer, M. (1975): *Working Class Images of Society* (London: Routledge and Kegan Paul).

Chakrabarty, D. (1984): "Trade Unions in a Hierarchical Culture: The Jute Workers of Calcutta, 1920-50" in R. Guha (ed.) *Subaltern Studies*, Vol. 3 (New Delhi: OUP).

—— (1985): "Invitation to a Dialogue" in R. Guha (ed.) *Subaltern Studies*, Vol. 4 (New Delhi: OUP).

—— (1991): "History as Critique and Critique(s) of History", *Economic and Political Weekly*, Vol. XXVI, No. 37, September 14.

—— (1995): "Radical Histories and the Question of Enlightenment Rationalism: Some Recent Critiques of Subaltern Studies", *Economic and Political Weekly*, Vol. XXX, No. 14, April 8.

Chaturvedi, V. (ed.) (2012): *Mapping Subaltern Studies and the Postcolonial* (London: Verso).

Chatterjee, P. (1982): "Agrarian Relations and Communalism in Bengal,

1926-1935" in R. Guha (ed.) *Subaltern Studies,* Vol. 1 (New Delhi: OUP).

—— (1983): "Peasants, Politics and Historiography: A Response", *Social Scientist*, Vol. 11, No. 120, May.

—— (1985): "Modes of Power: Some Clarifications", *Social Scientist*, No. 141, February.

—— (1989): "Caste and Subaltern Consciousness" in R. Guha (ed.) *Subaltern Studies,* Vol. 6 (New Delhi: OUP).

—— (2009): "Editor's Introduction" to R. Guha, *The Small Voice of History* (Ranikhet: Permanent Black).

—— (2011): "Democracy and Economic Transformation" in *Lineages of Political Society* (Ranikhet: Permanent Black).

—— (2012a): "The Nation and its Peasants" in V. Chaturvedi (ed.).

—— (2012b): "After Subaltern Studies", *Economic and Political Weekly*, Vol. XLVII, No. 35, September 1.

—— (2013): "Subaltern Studies and Capital", *Economic and Political Weekly,* Vol. XLVIII, No. 37, September 14.

Chibber, V. (2013): *Post Colonial Theory and the Spectre of Capital* (New Delhi: Navayana).

—— (2014): "Revisiting Subaltern Studies", *Economic and Political Weekly*, Vol. XLIX, No. 9, March 1.

Connerton, P. (1974): "The Collective Historical Subject—Reflections on Lukacs' History and Class Consciousness," *The British Journal of Sociology*, 26, 2, June.

Dhanagare, D.N. (1993): "Subaltern Consciousness and Populism: Two Approaches in the Study of Social Movements in India", Chapter 6, in *Themes and Perspectives in Indian Sociology* (New Delhi: Rawat Publications).

Dirlik, A. (1994): "The Postcolonial Aura: Third World Criticism in the Age of Global Capitalism", *Critical Inquiry*, Vol. 20, No. 2, Winter.

Economic and Political Weekly, Special Correspondent, "The Subaltern in South Asian History and Society: Report of a Conference", *Economic and Political Weekly*, Vol. 18, No. 9, February 26.

Goldmann, L. (1971): in I. Meszaros (ed.), *Aspects of History and Class Consciousness* (London: Routledge and Kegan Paul).

Gramsci, A. (1971): *Selection from the Prison Notebooks of Antonio Gramsci*, in Q. Hoare and G.N. Smith (eds.), (London: Lawrence and Wishart).

Guha, R. (1982): "Preface" and "On Some Aspects of Historiography of Colonial India", in R. Guha (ed.) *Subaltern Studies*, Vol. 1 (New Delhi: OUP).

—— (1983 a): "The Prose of Counter-Insurgency" in R. Guha (ed.): *Subaltern Studies*, Vol. 3 (New Delhi: OUP).

—— (1983 b): *Elementary Aspects of Peasant Insurgency in Colonial India* (Delhi: OUP).

—— (1989): "Dominance Without Hegemony and its Historiography" in R. Guha (ed.) *Subaltern Studies*, Vol. 6 (Delhi: OUP).

—— (1992): "Discipline and Mobilize" in P. Chatterjee and G. Pandey (eds.) *Subaltern Studies*, Vol. 7 (Delhi: OUP).

—— (1996): "The Small Voice of History" in S. Amin and D. Chakrabarty (eds.) *Subaltern Studies*, Vol. 9 (Delhi: OUP).

—— (1998): "An Indian Historiography of India: Hegemonic Implications of a Nineteenth-Century Agenda" in *Dominance without Hegemony: History and Power in Colonial India* (Delhi: OUP).

Guha, R. (ed.) (2000): *A Subaltern Studies Reader* (Delhi: OUP).

Gupta, D. (1985): "On Altering the Ego in Peasant History: Paradoxes of the Ethnic Option", *Journal of Peasant Studies*, 13 (1).

Gupta, R.D. (1996): "Indian Working Class and Some Recent Historiographical Issues", *Economic and Political Weekly*, Vol. XXXI, No. 8, February 24.

Guru, G. and S. Sarukkai (2013): *The Cracked Mirror: An Indian Debate on Experience and Theory* (New Delhi: OUP).

Hardiman, D. (1986): "Subaltern Studies at Crossroads", *Economic and Political Weekly*, Vol. XXI, No. 7, February 15.

—— (ed.) (1993): *Peasant Resistance in India, 1858-1914* (Delhi: OUP).

—— (1994): "Power in the Forests: The Dangs 1820-1940" in D. Arnold and D. Hardiman (ed.) *Subaltern Studies*, Vol. 8 (Delhi: OUP).

Harvey, D. (1990): *The Condition of Postmodernity* (Cambridge MA and Oxford UK: Blackwell).

Haynes, D. and G. Prakash (eds.) (1991): *Contesting Power: Resistance and Everyday Social Relations in South Asia* (Delhi: OUP).

Ilaih, K. (1996): "Productive Labour, Consciousness and History: The Dalitbahujan Alternative" in S. Amin and D. Chakrabarty (eds.) *Subaltern Studies,* Vol. 9 (Delhi: OUP).

Kumar, K. and others:"Subaltern Studies III & IV: A Review Article", *Social Scientist*, Vol. 16, No. 3, March.

Lehmann, D. (1972): "Peasant Consciousness and Agrarian Reforms in Chile", *The European Journal of Sociology,* 13, 2.

Lockwood, D. (1966): "Sources of Variation in Working Class Images of Society," *Sociological Review,* 14, 3, November.

Loomba, A. (1998): *Colonialism/Post-colonialism* (London: Routledge).

Lucacs, G. (1971): *History and Class Consciousness* in R. Livingstone (trans.) (London: Merlin Press).

Ludden, D. (ed.) (2002): *Reading Subaltern Studies: Critical History, Contested Meaning and the Globalization of South Asia* (London: Anthem Press).

Maggio, J. (2007): "Can the Subaltern Be Heard?: Political Theory, Translation, Representation, and Gayatri Chakravorty Spivak", *Alternatives* 32.

Mallon, F.E. (1994): "The Promise and Dilemma of Subaltern Studies: Perspectives from Latin American History", *The American Historical Review*, Vol. 99, No. 5, December.

Marx, K. and F. Engels (1976): *The German Ideology* (Moscow: Progress Publishers).

Marx, K. (1977): *Preface to the Critique of Political Economy,* in *Marx-Engels: Selected Works,* Vol. 1 (Moscow: Progress Publishers).

Marx, K. (1980): *The Holy Family* (Moscow: Progress Publishers).

Mann, M. (1973): *Consciousness and Action in the Western Working Class* (London: Macmillan).

Masselos, J. (2002): "The Disappearance of Subalterns: A Reading of a Decade of Subaltern Studies" in D. Ludden (ed.).

O'Hanlon, R. (1988): "Recovering the Subject: Subaltern Studies and Histories of Resistance in Colonial South Asia", *Modern Asian Studies*, Vol. 22, No. 1.

O'Hanlon, R. and D. Washbrook (1992): "After Orientalism: Culture, Criticism, and Politics in the Third World", *Comparative Studies in Society and History*, 34, 1.

Ollman, B. (1972): "Towards Class Consciousness Next Time: Marx and the Working Class", *Politics and Society*, Fall.

—— (1976): *Alienation: Marx's Conception of Man in Capitalist Society* (Cambridge: Cambridge University Press).

Pandey, G. (1991): "In Defense of the Fragment: Writing about Hindu-Muslim Riots in India Today", *Economic and Political Weekly*, Annual Number, Vol. XXVI, No. 11-12.

—— (1994): "The Prose of Otherness" in D. Arnold and D. Hardiman (eds.) *Subaltern Studies*, Vol. 8 (Delhi: OUP).

—— (2012 a): "Un-archived Histories: The 'Mad' and the 'Trifling'", *Economic and Political Weekly*, Vol. XLVII, No. 1, January 7.

—— (2012 b): "Voices from the Edge: The Struggle to Write Subaltern Histories" in V. Chaturvedi (ed.).

Parthasarthi, P. (2003): "The State of Indian Social History", *Journal of Social History*, Vol. 37, No. 1, Autumn.

Prakash, G. (1994): "Subaltern Studies as Postcolonial Criticism", *The American Historical Review*, Vol. 99, No. 5, December.

—— (2012 a): "Writing Post-Orientalist Histories of the Third World: Perspectives from Indian Historiography" in V. Chaturvedi (ed.).

—— (2012 b): "Can the 'Subaltern Ride'? A Reply to O'Hanlon and Washbrook" in V. Chaturvedi (ed.).

Prasad, S. (1985): "Modes of Power: Some Ambiguities", *Social Scientist*, Vol. 13, No. 151, December.

Prashad, V. (1999): "Untouchable Freedom: A Critique of the Bourgeois Landlord Indian State" in G. Bhadra and others (eds.) *Subaltern Studies*, Vol. 10 (Delhi: OUP).

Rao, A. (2005): "Death of a Kotwal: Injury and the Politics of Recognition" in S. Mayaram, M.S.S. Pandian and A. Skaria (eds.) *Subaltern Studies*, Vol. 12 (Ranikhet: Permanent Black).

Sabin, M. (2008): "In Search of Subaltern Consciousness", *Prose Studies: History, Theory, Criticism*, Vol. 30, No. 2, August.

Saldanha, D. (1984): "A Socio-Psychological Study of the Development of Class Consciousness", Ph.D. Thesis, Mumbai, Department of Sociology, University of Bombay, August 1984.

—— (1988): "Antonio Gramsci and the Analysis of Class Consciousness: Some Methodological Considerations", *Economic and Political Weekly,* Review of Political Economy, Vol. 23, No. 5, January 30.

—— (1989): "Socialisation of Critical Thought: Responses to Illiteracy Among the Adivasis in Thane District", *Economic and Political Weekly,* Review of Political Economy, Vol. 24, No. 30, July 29.

—— (1993): "Cultural Communication in Literacy Campaigns: Social Relational Contexts, Processes and Hegemonic Organisation", *Economic and Political Weekly,* Vol. 28, No. 20, May 15.

—— (1999): "Residual Illiteracy and Uneven Development: 1) Patterned Concentration of Literacy, 2) Literacy and Development Characteristics, 3) Performance of Literacy Campaigns and Prospects", *Economic and Political Weekly,* Vol. 34, Nos. 27, 28, 29; July 3, 10, 17.

—— (2007): *Education of Adolescents for Development in India: The Case of Doosra Dashak* (Jaipur: Rawat Publications).

—— (2008 a): "Consciousness and Structure in the Gramscian Perspective: Conceptual Concerns", *Contemporary Education Dialogue*, Vol. 6, No. 1, Monsoon.

—— (2008 b): "Consciousness and Structure in the Gramscian Perspective: Implications for Education". *Contemporary Education Dialogue*, Vol. 6, No. 1, Monsoon.

—— (2010): *Civil Society Processes and the State: The BGVS and the Literacy Campaigns* (Jaipur, Rawat Publications).

—— (2015): *Structure, Consciousness and Social Transformation: The Adivasis in Thane District, Maharashtra* (Delhi: Aakar Books).

Sarkar, S. (1984): "The Condition and Nature of Subaltern Militancy: Bengal from Swadeshi to Non-Cooperation, c. 1905-22" in R. Guha (ed.) *Subaltern Studies,* Vol. 3 (Delhi: OUP).

—— (1997 a): *Writing Social History* (Delhi: OUP).

—— (1997 b): "The Many Worlds of Indian History" in Sarkar, S. (1997a).

—— (1997 c): "The Relevance of E.P. Thompson" in Sarkar, S. (1997a).

—— (1997 d): "The Decline of the Subaltern in Subaltern Studies" in Sarkar, S. (1997 a).

—— (1997 e): "Identity and Difference: Caste in the Formation of the Ideologies of Nationalism and Hindutva" in Sarkar, S. (1997 a).

—— (2012): "Orientalism Revisited: Saidian Frameworks in the Writing of Modern Indian History" in V. Chaturvedi (ed.).

Sen, A. (1987): "Subaltern Studies: Capital, Class and Community", in R. Guha (ed.), *Subaltern Studies,* Vol. 5 (New Delhi: OUP).

Sivaramakrishnan, K. (2002): "Situating the Subaltern: History and Anthropology in the Subaltern Studies Project" in D. Ludden (ed.).

Siddiqi, M.H. (1985): "Review of Ranajit Guha (ed.) Subaltern Studies Vol. 3", *Indian Economic and Social History Review*, 22:92.

Simon, R. (1977): "Gramsci's Concept of Hegemony", *Marxism Today,* 21(3).

Skaria, A. (1996): "Writing, Orality and Power in the Dangs", in S. Amin and D. Chakrabarty (eds.), *Subaltern Studies,* Vol. 9 (New Delhi: OUP).

—— (1999): "Some Aporias of History: Time, Truth and Play in Dangs, Gujarat", *Economic and Political Weekly*, Vol. XXXIV, No. 15, April 10.

Spivak, G. (1988): "Can the Subaltern Speak?" in C. Nelson and L. Grossberg (eds.), *Marxism and the Interpretation of Culture* (Basingstoke: Macmillan Education).

Thompson, E.P. (1968): *The Making of the English Working Class* (London: Pelican Books).

—— (1978): "Eighteenth-Century English Society: Class Struggle Without Class?", *Social History,* Vol. 3, No. 2, May.

—— (2010): *The Poverty of Theory* (Delhi: Aakar Books).

Westergaard, J.H. (1970): "The Rediscovery of the Cash Nexus", *Socialist Register*.

Index